Workers' Councils: The Yugoslav Experience

Workers' Councils

The Yugoslav Experience

JIRI KOLAJA

FREDERICK A. PRAEGER, Publishers

NEW YORK · WASHINGTON

1966

BOOKS THAT MATTER

Published in the United States of America in 1966
by Frederick A. Praeger, Inc., Publishers
111 Fourth Avenue, New York, 3, N.Y.

Printed in Great Britain

Contents

Acknowledgements

The author would like to express his appreciation, for their critical comments on the manuscript, to Dr William F. Whyte of Cornell University and to Mrs M. Poček-Matić of Institut za Društveno Upravljanje NRH, Zagreb. Thanks are also due to the University of Kentucky Research Fund and the Social Science Research Council for financial help; to Institut Društvenih Nauka and Savezni Zavod za Produktivnost Rada for their cooperation; to Mr S. Stojanović for assistance in the field work; to Mrs Russell S. Moore for typing the manuscript; and to Dr Thomas B. Stroup and Miss Shirley M. Baker of the English Department of the University of Kentucky for editorial assistance.

Introduction

Yugoslavia occupies a unique position in the world today. This has come about not only as a result of its policy of non-alignment in the political struggle between West and East, but also as a consequence of certain internal developments that have taken place in the country since 1950. Yugoslavia has carried out a vigorous search for some sort of equilibrium between the processes of central planning, central decision-making, and national enforcement, and the processes that serve to strengthen and develop the autonomy of smaller political and economic units. Whereas in the United States, for example, the overall trend has been to increase the role of federal government, in Yugoslavia, which in 1945 had a highly centralized and all-embracing system of political and economic controls, the trend since 1950 has been gradually to reduce the role of federal agencies.

Furthermore, because it was at the same time experimenting with new forms of economic organization, Yugoslavia, which in the years 1934 to 1938 had a consumption level below those of Cuba, Spain, and Mexico, had naturally become of great interest to the emerging underdeveloped nations of Africa and Asia.[1] Here is a European nation whose problems of economic development and political integration were more or less similar to those of the new struggling nations. For not only was Yugoslavia economically backward, but its struggle for political independence, linked with the need to reduce powerful local conflicts of nationality and religion, resembled the anti-colonial liberation movements and the integrative efforts of these new nations, some of which are still torn apart by local tribal loyalties. Though these countries could not expect significant

[1] Bennett (1951).

ix

economic help from Yugoslavia, they could learn from its experiences and solutions.[1]

Economic and political changes, which are taking place with increasing frequency as new nations emerge, have, of course, attracted the attention of social scientists. Combining a cross-cultural comparative approach with theories of economic development – which, incidentally, are not very different in form from nineteenth-century theories of evolution – economists such as Kerr, Dunlop, Harbison, Myers, and Rostow have developed interpretations of industrialization, focusing especially upon its universal variables.[2] For example, within a context of the comparative analysis of work regulations, Dunlop has devoted a chapter of his book *Industrial Relations Systems* to the Yugoslav case (1959, pp. 264–306).

In studying social phenomena which are not directly accessible, social scientists have relied for their data upon indirect indices such as legal codes, official statistics, reports of occasional travellers, and descriptions by former nationals of the countries concerned. Since no official sociological research has been conducted in Communist countries until recently, social scientists living in those countries have had little more, in some instances even less, information than their colleagues in the West.

Fortunately, sociological research has been introduced into Yugoslavia in recent years, and applied among other things to the study of the new economic organization which is also the object of this investigation – namely, the workers' council. Two studies, one by Poček (1960) and the other by Brekić (1961), have analysed the turnover of members of the workers' council. Attitudes towards supervisors and the distribution of profits have been analysed by Sinadinović (1959) and Radosavljević (1961). Ničković (1961) has studied to what extent workers are informed about organizational structure. And a method of content analysis has been applied to workers' council agenda as

[1] During the years of Algeria's struggle for independence, Yugoslav newspapers frequently drew analogies between the Yugoslav partisan movement of the second world war and Algerian military efforts.

[2] Dunlop (1959); Kerr, Dunlop, Harbison & Myers (1960); Rostow (1960).

reported in newspapers (Šušnić, 1961) and to minutes of workers' council meetings (Tanić, 1961).[1] In the subsequent report references will be made occasionally to the Yugoslav research findings.

The study presented here was undertaken in the summer of 1959 in Belgrade, aided by a research grant from the Social Science Research Council, which, of course, cannot be held accountable for any of the opinions or weaknesses displayed in this report. Two Yugoslav organizations, Institut Društvenih Nauka (Social Science Institute) and Savezni Zavod za Produktivnost Rada (Federal Institute of Productivity) helped me to obtain permission to carry out research in two factories.[2] Mr Svetozar Stojanović from the University of Belgrade assisted me for some time in the field work.

Originally, it was planned to study only one factory (Factory A) over a period of two months. However, as a result of the unfortunate intervention of the director of Factory A in the research, it became necessary to limit my collection of data there to two sources: attendance at formal meetings and content analysis of the minutes of earlier meetings. To overcome this situation, therefore, I decided to move to another factory (Factory B); here I was able to administer a questionnaire, which I could not do satisfactorily in Factory A.[3] Factory A had been selected for me by the Federal Institute of Productivity; in the

[1] An extensive study of several workers' councils in the town of Varaždin has recently appeared (Matić, Poček & Bosanac; see *Industrial and Labor Relations Review*, January 1964, pp. 338–9, for my review of this book).

[2] When I visited the factories again for a few days in the summer of 1961, I showed parts of this report in prepublication form to the director of Factory B and to the new director of Factory A; the latter had been head of the machine-maintenance section in Factory A at the time of my research there in 1959. Interestingly enough, they made practically no comments on the report.

[3] It should be made clear that the difference between Factory A and Factory B as far as the collection of the data is concerned is that in Factory A I interviewed persons informally concerning their degree of knowledge about the activities of the workers' council, whereas in Factory B this and other information was collected by means of a questionnaire. In both factories I was able to attend meetings and to analyse the minutes of former meetings.

case of Factory B I would emphasize not only that I was free to select the factory myself, but also that I was fortunate enough to get the cooperation of the director there and of the local workers' council.

I was able to turn the fact of having to move to a second factory to some advantage by letting the research develop rather as a comparison of two workers' councils than as a single case study. Nevertheless, because of the unexpected move and many consequent improvisations, and also because I spent only about four weeks in each factory, the study can easily be criticized from the methodological viewpoint. In general, the method used consisted of observation and semi-structured interviewing combined with the content analysis of personnel files and minutes of former meetings.[1] The questionnaire has already been reported upon elsewhere (Kolaja, 1961), and I shall only summarily refer to its results.

In addition to comparing the two workers' councils, the study examines the constitution and role of the managerial group in each factory, and of the factory branches of the League of Communists, the labour union, and the youth organization. The workers' councils operated in relation to these four other organizations, constituting with them a structure of five major organized groups within each enterprise.

The material is presented in the following way: First, there is a brief survey and discussion of the legislation concerning workers' councils. This is followed by a general description of the two factories, and an account of their workers' councils, labour union committees, youth organizations, and League of Communists organizations – as derived from written records. Third is the presentation of selected data gathered at first hand through attendance at meetings, observation, and informal contacts of various kinds. In conclusion, the evidence from all sources is related and theoretically interpreted. There is also some discussion of Dunlop's evaluation of the Yugoslav workers' council.

---

[1] I used the same combination of observational and analytical data in my earlier study, *A Polish Factory* (1960).

ONE

The Yugoslav Workers' Council

The present unique position of Yugoslavia within South-Eastern Europe and its relation with the Soviet Union cannot well be understood without reflection upon the events of the second world war. Yugoslavia was the only European country which, though completely overrun by the Axis forces, succeeded in regaining some parts of its territory and in keeping them under partisan control for the remainder of the war. The strong Yugoslav partisan movement left its imprint also upon the Yugoslav Communist Party. A visitor to the Kalemegdan 'Museum of the Liberation Struggle' in Belgrade, who reads the war appeals that were issued by Tito and his commanders, can hardly fail to notice their strong emphasis upon national independence. The Yugoslav partisans were fighting primarily 'for their country', and only secondarily, and to a far lesser extent, for the distant goals of world communism. In consequence, the political break with Moscow and the Cominform which occurred in 1948 should not have been a surprising occurrence.

Along with the Yugoslavs' desire to achieve political independence outside the sphere of Soviet influence was their increasing tendency to experiment in their own way with new economic and political institutions. Though Yugoslav publications explain the transition from the so-called state administration of the national economy to the new decentralized system of workers' councils as being a result of economic developments that had taken place in the years 1945–49,[1] it seems that the

[1] See Information Service Yugoslavia, 'The Development of Workers' Self-government', p. 3; Kovač (1958, p. 5). The Basic Law relating to the Management of State Economic Enterprises on the part of the Working Collectives was issued on 28 June 1950.

change in the international situation was also a contributing factor. The growing trend in Yugoslavia to emphasize local administration and to decrease the power of the state was introduced partly, it appears, to serve as an ideological weapon against the Stalinist central monopoly of power.[1] In several Yugoslav publications issued since 1950, the Marxist theme of the 'withering away of the state' has been stressed and skilfully employed. It is stated that the primary unit of self-government is the territorial unit of the community called the commune. The persons who live and work within the boundaries of the local commune are responsible for making the decisions on economic, educational, health, recreational, and other matters for the area. Only when the local commune is unable to solve a problem are bodies covering larger territorial units to be called upon: these are district, republican, and finally federal assemblies.

To underline the decreasing role of the state, enterprises are defined not as state property, but as social property. On the other hand, workers in the enterprise are entitled to 'manage' it but not to own it. In the basic law it is stated that 'the working collective shall manage as the people's property, and in the name of society, the factories, mines, means of communication, means of transportation, and commercial, agricultural, forest, communal, and other socially owned economic enterprises, and they shall do so within the framework of the state economic plan and pursuant to the rights and duties as established by the laws and other legal prescriptions' (Deleon, 1956, p. 20, note 2).[2]

What does it mean if an enterprise is defined as 'the people's property'? In what way is a production unit related to the local

---

[1] Notice also the change of name from 'Communist Party of Yugoslavia' to 'Federation of Yugoslav Communists'; that state ownership is characterized as 'a primitive socialist form of ownership' as compared with a system in which the producers themselves become managers (Sirotović, 1954, pp. 59–60); and that stress is laid on the ideological differences between the Yugoslav programme and Soviet communism in the *Program Związku Komunistów Jugosławii* (1959, pp. 52 and 55). Dunlop (1959, pp. 282–3) also points out that the role of ideology is much greater in Yugoslavia than in the more pragmatic British, United States, and Scandinavian societies.

[2] For a critical analysis of the basic law, see Adamovitch (1956, 1957).

commune and to the wider society? Following the setting up of workers' councils, another organization was introduced, the Council of Producers.[1] It too was established on communal, district, republican, and federal levels. The Councils of Producers are elected only by persons gainfully employed.[2] The local Council of Producers is entitled to inspect the operations of an enterprise. The enterprise sends periodical economic reports to the Council of Producers which, as an agency of the communal council, sends back 'recommendations concerning future policies'.[3] Procedures to be used if no agreement is reached on the part of the enterprise and the local Council of Producers are still being worked out. There is, however, a strong emphasis upon the advisory character of communications sent to the enterprise by higher authorities.[4]

In addition to the relations with the local commune and the

[1] See Djordjević and Pašić (1961).

[2] Though persons engaged in agriculture constituted 75 per cent of the working population by 1953, only 31 per cent of the delegates at the Federal Assembly of Producers were farmers or people in related occupations. This disproportionate representation was explained in terms of the differential contributions of particular occupational groups to the total national income. According to Deleon (1956, p. 30), industry and services contributed 66 per cent, and agriculture no more than 31 per cent, of the national income. Note, however, that by 1960 equal proportions of the population were engaged in agricultural and in industrial occupations. See Tito's speech reported in *Borba* (Belgrade), 19 April 1960, p. 2.

[3] The commune-enterprise relationship was defined by Gligorov (1961) as follows: (i) the commune sometimes provides financial funds for the enterprise, which cooperates with the communal council in providing for the educational and public health needs of the local population; (ii) the commune supervises the distribution of profits made by the enterprise, and audits the annual accounts. 'Although the enterprise is under no legal obligation to follow the commune's recommendations, the political and moral influence is considerable' (p. 413).

[4] According to Kovač and Miljević (1958, p. 162) the relationship is broadly defined as a 'control concerning the observation of the legal limits within which the enterprise is supposed to operate'. The director of Factory B defined the relationship as follows: 'The workers' council is obliged to consider and discuss recommendations but it is not bound to accept them. The workers' council's obligation is political rather than legal.'

3

larger society that are maintained by means of the Councils of Producers, there are four ways by which an enterprise is related to, or controlled by, society.

First, the director of the enterprise is appointed by a communal committee composed of members of the enterprise and representatives of the commune. The director is responsible to the workers' council for the implementation of its decisions, but he is also responsible to the community. Second, the enterprise is controlled to a considerable degree by the market. Though competition between manufacturers is not extended to all products, generally speaking there is a free market in Yugoslavia today; thus, if a firm does not dispose of its products, it will suffer financial loss. Third, along with the control effected by the market goes the credit control exercised by banks which might, under certain conditions, refuse to grant credit to the enterprise. Fourth, the enterprise is related to society by industrial chambers and by industrial and professional associations. The chambers for particular industries are authorized by law, and in some industries membership of them is obligatory; professional associations on the other hand are created by the enterprises themselves.[1] The purpose of these bodies is to assist the enterprise in its activities, for example in technological research and innovation, and in the establishment of commercial relations with other countries. The chambers also function as arbitrators on 'fair competition' practices, though not, as Dunlop reports (1959, p. 298), on prices.

Turning to the enterprise itself, let us describe first the structure of relations between the workers' council and the other organizations that operate within the factory. Usually five organizations are involved; and if the managing board of the workers' council is counted as a separate body, there are six groups. These are, in addition to the workers' council and its managing board, the managerial group; the League of Communists; the labour union, called by Yugoslavs the syndicate; and the youth organization, called *omladina*. It should be noted that

[1] *Yugoslav Facts and Views*, 'Statute of enterprises in Yugoslavia' (1957, pp. 6–7).

the League of Communists, the labour union, and the youth organization, through their communal, republican, and federal organizational units, make up three additional links between the enterprise and the society.

As far as functions are concerned, the League of Communists' role is described as educational;[1] the Communist organization thus remains in the background. Activities connected with the management and the social life of the factory are primarily undertaken by the workers' council, the labour union, and management. Each new workers' council is initiated by the labour union, which organizes the elections in the enterprise. Once elected, the workers' council in turn elects its executive body, i.e. the managing board, on which the director is a member *ex officio*. The managing board periodically reports its activities to the workers' council. The labour union participates occasionally in meetings organized by the workers' council, helping in particular with problems concerning the training and morale of workers.[2] A good indication of the way in which these organizations interlock is given by the fact that all of them send delegates to the workers' council, or have members who participate also in the council's activities. Even the youth organization, of which little has been said because of its relative lack of influence on the management of the factory, is represented on the workers' council.

The basic relationship in the management of an enterprise is that between the workers' council and the director: the workers' council directs and guides the enterprise (*upravljanje*); the director manages it (*rukovodjenje*).[3] The general duties of the workers' council have sometimes been compared to those of a board of trustees, or to the controls exercised by shareholders, because the

[1] See, for example, Bogosavljević and Pešaković (1959, p. 102) and *Program Związku Komunistów Jugosławii* (1959, p. 210).

[2] In the preamble to the statute of the Yugoslav labour unions of 14 May 1955 there is only a brief reference to the protection of workers' interests, though there is some elaboration of the subject of workers' education (see Adamovitch, 1956, p. 331).

[3] See the differentiation and definition of the two terms in Rašković (1961).

director is responsible to the workers' council for the execution of its decisions. More specifically, together with the communal representatives, the workers' council selects and appoints the managing director and executive directors. It approves production, wage, and marketing policies and plans; rules of conduct; and reports submitted by the managing board; it decides how that part of the earnings which is left to the disposal of the enterprise is to be distributed. As has already been stated, the council elects its managing board, which acts as its executive body. In general, the workers' council is entitled to be concerned with every problem of the enterprise. It is also the highest authority in the enterprise to which persons can appeal.

The duties of the director are defined as work organization, the implementation of decisions taken by the workers' council, and the observation and enforcement of the legal prescriptions;[1] he also represents the enterprise in relation to other enterprises and to governmental bodies.

The managing board's duties are more specific than those of the workers' council. Up to a certain point, the managing board can dispose of financial matters without waiting for the consent of the workers' council. The board handles personnel problems, specifies wage and production norms, promotes the vocational advancement of workers (note that the same duty is ascribed to the labour union), sets out the monthly plan of the enterprise, seeks to increase productivity, and appoints employees to executive positions. Whereas the workers' council usually meets once a month, the managing board usually meets weekly or, if necessary, even more frequently.

Considering the legal framework as such, the division of rights and duties between the workers' council, the managing board,

---

[1] The director can refuse to implement a policy decision if he thinks that it contradicts standing legal norms. If a conflict arises between the director and the workers' council, the matter is brought before the communal Council of Producers. Dunlop (1959, p. 291) lists also the recruitment of labour as one of the director's duties. In the factories that I studied recruitment was transferred to special committees composed of workers' council and labour union members.

6

and the director and his managerial group displays similarities with democratic governmental institutions. The problematic difference that remains, however, is whether there is provision, within the existing framework, for the organization of an opposition. Yugoslav theoreticians would say that everyone is free to lodge complaints with the managerial board, or to voice dissent at meetings of the workers' council or of the labour union. As far as the opportunity to strike is concerned, the answer would be that 'nobody strikes against himself' (Deleon, 1956, p. 90). Since the workers or producers have become also the managers of the business, strikes are considered out of place. Thus the labour union is also described as having an educational role: in the first place it supports the management, and in the second place it is the workers' welfare organization.

If the workers are to identify with the workers' council, the election of the council is important. As legally set forth, everyone in the enterprise who is over eighteen years old has the right to vote.[1] The candidates are usually proposed by the factory labour union; however, any other group can submit its own list of candidates, provided that it obtains the support of at least one-tenth of all the qualified voters. No doubt this provision makes it possible for an opposition to compete for votes, but any such group could be only on a temporary basis, without an organizational framework; hence its chances of survival or of winning the support of the majority seem slim.

In order to secure a fair representation on the workers' council of manual workers as compared with white-collar employees, it is directed that manual workers be proportionally represented

[1] If an enterprise has fewer than thirty workers, all will be members of the workers' council. In larger enterprises, councils range in size from a minimum of fifteen members to a maximum of 120, elected for one year. The limit of 120 members is set in order to preserve the manageability of the deliberating body. The largest enterprises also have departmental workers' councils, which send delegates to the main council. Departmental workers' councils were introduced in the electrical equipment factory Rade Končar in Zagreb in 1955. The enterprise had about 3,800 employees in 1957 (see Bogosavljević and Pešaković, 1959, pp. 53 and 92). The establishment of departmental workers' councils is left to the discretion of the enterprise.

among candidates. As far as their participation in the managing board is concerned, the law states that three-quarters of the members (the board can have between three and eleven members) must be directly employed on the production line.[1] The director is an *ex officio* member of the managerial board, but not of the workers' council, to which he cannot be elected. Though it is not spelled out legally, there seems to be a general expectation that none of the other executives can be elected to the chairmanship of either the workers' council or the managing board.[2] To protect the members of the managing board from the possibility of hostile action by the director, the law stipulates that, during his tenure of a seat on the board, an individual cannot be relieved of his employment, nor transferred to another position within the enterprise.

Another interesting point is that the law provides for the turnover of persons within the workers' council and the managing board.[3] Only one-third of the managing board can be reappointed for a consecutive year, and no one can serve for three years in succession. There has been discussion concerning the establishment of a standardized procedure for the turnover of workers' council delegates.[4] Whatever the final outcome may be, the legislation is based on the idea of increasing the number of workers who would serve on the workers' council. Obviously,

[1] For a detailed description of the legal prescriptions, see Kovač and Miljević (1958, pp. 68–77). (The stipulation that three-quarters of the members must be production workers applies explicitly to the managing board, not to the whole workers' council as erroneously stated by Dunlop, 1959, p. 287.)

[2] Kovač and Miljević (1958, pp. 79–80) point out that there is some uncertainty whether any executives ought even to be considered as eligible for membership of the workers' council. In the two factories studied, managerial staff were elected members of both the council and the managing board, but none of them was chairman.

[3] By 1958–59 one-third of the total number of workers were reported to have passed through workers' councils as members (see Horvat and Rašković, 1959, p. 195).

[4] Kovač and Miljević report one suggestion that the term of membership of the workers' council should be two years, with one-half of the delegates elected each year. This would bring about a considerable circulation and yet preserve continuity of the body (see Kovač and Miljević, 1958, pp. 81–2).

8

the major reason for this emphasis upon the turnover of delegates is the educational function that the council at present has to fulfil.

The workers' council regulations include the provision of compensation for workers for time spent in sessions of the deliberating bodies; it is also laid down, among other things, that the simple majority of those present prevails (but at least one-half of the total membership must be present); and that all decisions have to be taken at sessions (only the director is not bound by this rule).

To conclude this section, let us consider an item in the regulations that is of great importance, namely, the sharing in the profits of the enterprise. Yugoslav theoreticians assume that profit-sharing will be the most significant factor for turning producer-employees into managers.

In the foregoing discussion of the relations between the enterprise and the community or the state, it has been pointed out that the Federal Council of Producers sets up certain economic or financial limits within which an enterprise is permitted to operate. In addition, the republican and the communal bodies prepare their regional or communal specifications. The basic and all-embracing instrument is the federal economic plan, within which it is roughly determined what proportions of the national income are to be spent on investment, what on savings, and what on consumption.[1] To illustrate some of the instruments by which the federal authorities regulate economic process in Yugoslavia, it may be said that they determine the rate of interest on fixed assets as well as the interest on working assets to be paid to the Investment Fund of the National Bank, and that they make prescriptions concerning amortisation funds, capital expenditure funds, etc. These rates of interest are applied on a differential basis according to whether the community or the larger political units desire to encourage particular fields of production or particular enterprises. There is also a tendency to equalize wage and profit levels among enterprises. Furthermore, there is a turnover

[1] According to Dunlop (1959, p. 277) the Yugoslav plan, in general outline, resembles an Indian rather than a Soviet plan.

9

tax by means of which the consumption of particular goods is encouraged or discouraged. It is clear that enterprises, in their endeavour to increase profits, react to changing rates of interest or to special preferential taxation in much the same way as enterprises in the West.

Provided that an enterprise is successful, the difference between gross returns on production and total expenses makes up the profit of the enterprise. From this profit a sum is taken by federal, republican, and communal profit taxes.[1] Obviously, this amount is also determined, and the enterprise does not have much say in the matter. However, as far as the reserve fund or capital investment funds are concerned, the federal plan only lays down limits within which it is for the workers' council to decide how the remainder of the profit will be distributed. Thus the workers' council decides what amount ought to be invested, or paid out as additional salaries, or spent on collective consumption projects such as new housing facilities, and so on.

One more provision should be mentioned here: if an enterprise makes no profit and closes the year with a loss, workers must still get 60 per cent of their average salaries. If the enterprise is unable to pay this sum from its reserve fund, the community has to furnish funds for at least two months, and the enterprise is placed under a newly appointed administration or another solution is found (Adamovitch, 1957, p. 176).[2]

Thus the worker's income is composed of two parts: the normal wage (60 per cent of which is guaranteed, if necessary, by the community), and a share in the profits of the enterprise, which is dependent on the collective effort of the whole enterprise. Recent developments have led to the introduction of so-called 'economic units', units of a maximum size of 120 per-

---

[1] For example, the Rade Končar enterprise in 1957 turned over approximately 62 per cent of its profits to the federal government and 8 per cent to the city of Zagreb (see Bogosavljević and Pešaković, 1959, p. 84). However, more recent changes have increased the share of the enterprise in the 'profit before taxes'.

[2] Dunlop (1959, pp. 299–300) reports that the commune guarantees 75 per cent of these payments.

sons; the economic unit keeps its own accounts, selling its work to or buying work from other economic units within the enterprise. This innovation is expected to reduce the gap between individual efforts and group rewards which, with a greater number of employed persons, is apt to widen.[1] In general, participation in the group reward is stressed by Yugoslav theoreticians as highly relevant for the development of the desired collective orientation of individual employees.[2]

In general, whereas the differential rates of interest granted to particular enterprises or to particular fields of production tend to reduce differences in profits among enterprises within the commune or the larger political units, the newly created economic unit tends to increase differences between production units within the factory. So far, then, the trend has been to increase the autonomy of the smaller territorial or production unit, though demands for coordination on a wider scale have also more recently been heard.[3] From the economic point of view, the workers' council and other internal developments have contributed to a considerable increase in production, but they do not explain it entirely.[4]

Second, if one is to characterize the new Yugoslav socio-economic system, one might appropriately call it a system of checks and balances, or, more adequately, a continuing search for the development of such a system. Some measures are designed to define an area within which the individual would be free to use his initiative in the management of a particular enterprise. The boundaries to such an area appear to be more effectively

[1] See several short comments under the title 'Razvoj i praksa ekonomskih jedinica', *Ekonomika preduzeća*, 1960 ,9, No. 1, pp. 39–41; No. 2, pp. 11–120. See also Županov and Marjanović (1960.)

[2] Kardelj (1957, p. 9).

[3] See 'Decentralization of Industry' in *Komunist* (Beograd), 9 July 1959, p. 1.

[4] The index of industrial production was 166 in 1951, when workers' councils were beginning to be established; by 1958, it was already 345 (Federal Statistical Institute, *Statistical Pocket-book of Yugoslavia 1959*, p. 52). Another important factor in Yugoslavia's expansion was Western, especially American, technical and material assistance. During the period 1948–54 Yugoslavia received $825 million from abroad (see Dunlop, 1959, p. 279).

established by financial measures than by legal prescriptions.[1] On the other hand, individual enterprises have opportunity to develop profitable schemes. It may be noted that the word 'profit' has become a reputable term again in Yugoslavia today.[2]

Third, along with experiments to discover the optimal limits within which both social control and individual drive for large profits would be integrated, goes the local decentralization embodied in the community or republican governments. The Yugoslav system could be described as the progressive encapsulation of smaller units by larger units, as the nature of the decisions becomes more general. It is found necessary to set limits within which the smaller units ought to operate, and to outline general signposts for the future economic development of the country.[3] There is a long-term economic plan, and likewise several annual operational plans, as well as a free market for most goods and for all labour.

Fourth, no doubt the Yugoslav system is original. On the one hand, Yugoslav theoreticians frequently stress that they are the 'true' heirs of Marx; on the other hand, Soviet theoreticians and their East European colleagues have, until recently, maintained that the Yugoslav system leads to anarchical economic conditions. Yugoslavs emphasize that in their system the locus of decision-making has been brought back to the factory, that the distance between managerial decisions and their implementation has been considerably shortened. Like Yugoslav authors, Dunlop points out that whereas stockholders are remote from managers

[1] Łukasz Winiarski reported a conversation with Kiro Gligorov, a leading figure in the Yugoslav Institute of Planning. Gligorov emphasized the greater effectiveness of economic measures as compared with 'administrative measures' (see 'List z Jugosławii', *Kultura* (Paris), January-February 1954, p. 119).

[2] To do justice to the Serbo-Croatian term *višak*, a more adequate translation would be 'surplus'.

[3] Choices between investment and consumption can pose certain 'encapsulation problems'. Eleanor Roosevelt reports that in a private conversation Tito expressed his disappointment that so many of the workers' councils did not allocate surpluses for the good of the community as a whole, but merely divided the funds among the workers (see Roosevelt, 1958, p. 195).

in Western corporations, the Yugoslav system in contrast has made managers responsible to employees who are directly selected from the workplace (1959, p. 284). Considered merely in terms of its legal-normative structure, the Yugoslav enterprise gives its employees considerably more opportunity to influence managerial decisions than is given to their counterparts in most Western enterprises. The question is, however, whether the opportunity written into legal-normative structure is realized on the functional-behaviouristic level. This problem will be examined in the following chapters, which present field-work data from two factories.

TWO

Two Factories and their Constituent Organizations

The two factories in which I was able to study the functioning of the workers' councils are referred to as Factory A and Factory B.

Factory A was a textile unit concentrating upon the production of cheap cotton material, similar to the factory I had previously studied in Poland (Kolaja, 1960, pp. 13–16). Before the second world war, it was owned by foreign capital. It was bombarded and immobilized during the 1941 German invasion of Yugoslavia. After the liberation of Belgrade – when the Yugoslav army occupied the city from the west and south, and Soviet units came from the east – the factory became state property. At the time of our research there were 1,620 employees, of whom approximately 20 per cent were men and 80 per cent women. It was reported that almost all the employees belonged to the labour union, and that about 15 per cent of them belonged to the League of Communists.

Factory B was created by the amalgamation of four smaller enterprises. Though organizationally united under one management, physically the four shops were apart, one of them being even beyond the city limits of Belgrade. It was planned to bring all the units to the main factory site where the management offices were located and the major part of the labour force was concentrated. The plant produced dyes and colours. At the time of our visit, there were 503 employees, of whom 66 per cent were men and 34 per cent women; 72 per cent belonged to the labour union, and about 12 per cent to the League of Communists.

Factory B employed a greater number of highly skilled personnel than Factory A, especially graduates in chemistry who worked in the research institute that constituted a part of the enterprise. Sixty persons, i.e. 12 per cent of all employees, had completed gymnasium, or were university graduates, or had at least attended university for some period of time; 316 persons were classified as manual workers (seventy-one as unskilled workers); and 187 as white-collar employees. Unfortunately the comparable data on education could not be obtained for Factory A.

In 1959 the workers' council in Factory A comprised fifty-nine members, and that in Factory B thirty-one. The managing boards, according to the legal norm, had eleven members each, including the director.[1]

The main outlines of the organizational structure of the two factories were as follows. Factory A had four departments: personnel, commercial, financial, and production-technical. This last department had five sectors: the technical bureau, the machine maintenance shop, the spinning shop, the weaving shop, and the finishing shop, which, because of their importance, were represented by their heads at all meetings of departmental heads. The nine heads of the four departments and the five sectors, together with the director, formed an informal managerial group called the 'collegium'. The group met at short notice from the director, frequently but irregularly.

Factory B had five departments: personnel, commercial, financial, technical, and the research institute. Though the five heads consulted with the director they were not identified by any

---

[1] Characteristic of the differences between the two factories was the difference in the educational background of the directors. The director of Factory A was a graduate of a textile high-school, and the director of Factory B a graduate of a college of chemistry. Director A, a single man in his fifties, had suffered poverty in childhood as an orphan. He had been a partisan. Director B was a single woman in her early forties, who came from a middle-class family in Belgrade. Both executives were members of the League of Communists. Possibly these differences between the two would partly explain why I fared better in my research in Factory B than in Factory A. Another reason may have been that the woman director was scheduled to visit the United States under the economic help programme offered by the United States to Yugoslavia.

title in Factory B. But Factory B had an assistant director, a position not found in Factory A.

The total income of Factory A for 1958 was about 2,500 million dinars, and of Factory B 2,630 million dinars. Whereas Factory A was able to pay only one-half of the monthly income to each employee as his share in the factory's profit, Factory B was considerably more successful financially: in 1958 each employee was rewarded with four extra monthly payments. Following up decisions of the workers' councils, both factories were constructing apartment houses for their employees.

Factory A and the main part of Factory B were situated in the same area of Belgrade, close to the Danube. There was room for future expansion, and both enterprises had long-range construction plans.

Each factory had a workers' council and a managing board; a labour union committee; a youth organization; and a League of Communists organization. I describe below the composition of these organizations, and the subjects that were dealt with at their meetings. Unfortunately, comparable data were not available on all points for both factories.

THE WORKERS' COUNCIL AND ITS MANAGING BOARD

What kind of persons are elected to the workers' council, and to its executive body, the managing board? *Tables 1* and *2* show the employment status of the council and board members in both factories, the number of women members, and how many members belonged to the League of Communists.

It will be seen from *Table 1* that skilled and semi-skilled workers form the largest group in the council in Factory A; in Factory B the managerial and white-collar group contributes the largest proportion of council members, followed by the skilled and semi-skilled group. The League of Communists is highly represented on the council in Factory A, with about 70 per cent of the council members belonging to the League. In Factory B less than half of the council members are also in the League of Communists.

TABLE 1 *Characteristics of the Workers' Council Members*
(Factories A and B, 1957–59)

Members	FACTORY A (1,620 workers in 1959)			FACTORY B (503 workers in 1959)		
	1957	*1958*	*1959*	*1957*	*1958*	*1959*
Total number	59	59	59	23	30	31
Managerial and white-collar	15	11	17	8	12	13
Highly skilled and foremen	5	6	10	6	7	7
Skilled and semi-skilled	36	34	32	9	11	11
Unskilled	3	2	0	0	0	0
Women	25	?	24	6	6	6
League of Communists	39	44	41	8	13	14

Note: The increase in the number of workers' council members in Factory B was due to the increase in the number of employees over the three years. The status of six members of the council in Factory A in 1958 could not be identified.

TABLE 2 *Characteristics of the Managing Board Members*
(Factories A and B, 1958–59)

Members	FACTORY A	FACTORY B
Total number	11	11
White-collar and managerial	4	3
Highly skilled and foremen	2	3
Skilled and semi-skilled	5	5
Women	4	2
League of Communists	7	4
Average age	33·5 years	37·9 years

Table 2 shows that the managing board personnel correspond roughly to the workers' council members in respect of employment status, except for the fact that skilled and semi-skilled workers are the largest group on the board in Factory B as well as in Factory A.

Some information was available for Factory B concerning the turnover of workers' council members. The 187 seats that were open to candidates during the years 1950–59 were filled by 111 persons, which means that several persons were elected to the council more than once. These data are presented in *Table 3*,

TABLE 3 *Re-election to Workers' Council*
(Factory B, 1950–59)

	Number of times elected				
	2	3	4	5	6
No. of persons	17	11	6	3	2
League of Communist members	4	3	2	None	None

which also shows how many of the re-elected members belonged to the League of Communists. It appears that those who served on the workers' council most frequently were not members of the League of Communists. This finding is consistent with the previous tables, which showed that League members were in the minority in the council in Factory B. On the other hand, in Factory A not only were the League's members in a majority on the council, but the director, a former partisan leader, tended to introduce political comments while dealing with economic affairs.

Brekić's study is of interest on this question of the relationship between membership of the League of Communists and the number of terms served on the workers' council. His findings indicate that individuals who are frequently re-elected to the councils are likely to be members of the League (Brekić, 1961,

18

p. 68).[1] This would suggest that Factory A with its larger representation of League members on the workers' council is more normal than Factory B with its relatively small proportion of Communists on the council.

From a study of the records of meetings, an attempt was made to analyse the sessions of the workers' councils and the management boards in the two factories, in terms of the frequency of participation of management and non-management members, the numbers of suggestions that were accepted from management and non-management levels, and the kinds of subject that were discussed. For this purpose, a method of content analysis was employed.

To measure frequency of participation in discussion, the name of the speaker listed in the minutes was counted as a unit; thus one participation could be either one sentence or several sentences. For a suggestion to be classified as accepted, there was usually a statement containing a verb such as 'accepted', 'passed', 'agreed', or 'approved'. If no such explicit expression was attached to a suggestion, the proposition was not counted as accepted. There were some accepted suggestions where the proposer was not identifiable from the context; such instances were classified separately.[2]

Management members had a higher participation score than non-management members in Factory A; whereas in Factory B,

[1] Brekić's study covered all enterprises in Varaždin, a town of 23,000 inhabitants in Croatia. However, he does not report how many enterprises were in fact involved.

[2] Essentially, the categorization of contents and the frequency of participation count must be considered as approximate only. I was the single 'judge', and I was obliged to work quickly when reading and analysing the minutes of former meetings. Furthermore, and this is even more detrimental to the desired objectivity of the content analysis method, minutes of meetings had not always been taken down by the same person, and no definite recording policies were established in either factory. For example, the total number of persons present was only sometimes reported. Thus the frequency of members' participation was calculated from their verbal participation as recorded in the minutes. Obviously not every verbal participation would be included, but it is probable that all agreed decisions were recorded. The data, then, are suggestive rather than evidential.

TABLE 4 *Frequency of Participation and Accepted Suggestions at the Workers' Council Sessions*

(Factories A and B)

	FACTORY A		FACTORY B [a]	
	17 sessions		22 sessions	
	16/4/57 to 7/4/58		24/4/57 to 9/4/58	
	Management personnel	Non-management personnel	Management personnel	Non-management personnel
Verbal participation	303	156	158	272
Accepted suggestions	49	18	71	47
Rejected suggestions	2	2	0	0

[a] For more detailed data on Factory B participation figures see Kolaja (1961, p. 23).

in contrast, there was more participation by non-management members (see *Table 4*). However, in both factories, as was expected, the majority of the accepted suggestions were proposed by management personnel.[1] Under 'management' were classified the director of each factory and the members of his collegium, regardless of whether they were simultaneously members of the current workers' council or were just invited to participate in meetings.

The greater frequency of verbal participation on the part of non-management personnel in Factory B's workers' council calls for further explanation. The chairman of the workers' council was a graduate engineer. There were also two university

[1] It should be added that, for Factory A, there were a further 56 accepted suggestions which have not been included in *Table 4* because it could not be determined from the records whether they should be attributed to management or non-management personnel.

graduates serving as members of the council. Since these three persons occupied research rather than top executive positions, they were listed under non-management. If their participation scores are subtracted from the total for the non-management members, the verbal participation score for Factory B non-management personnel falls to 186; similarly, the number of accepted suggestions is reduced to nine. Certainly this would indicate that, compared with persons of a lower standard of education, i.e. workers and foremen, management personnel and better-educated persons accounted for a large proportion of accepted suggestions.

Although the workers, foremen, and middle-level clerical personnel on Factory B's council had a higher verbal participation score than their counterparts on Factory A's council, they were responsible for a relatively lower number of accepted suggestions. A number of factors may contribute to this finding: (i) It may be a function of the size of the two councils. In a smaller body the rank-and-file members are more encouraged to speak. Not only was Factory B's workers' council smaller than Factory A's, but also everyone sat around one long table; whereas in Factory A the seating arrangement was that of a lecturer and an audience. (ii) There was a larger proportion of highly trained and well-educated persons on Factory B's council (see *Table 1*). (iii) The fact that the minutes of the two councils were recorded in different ways must also be taken into consideration. Thus the data for Factory B cover a greater number of sessions, yet the total frequency of participation score is smaller than in Factory A. The same holds true of the managing board sessions (see *Table 5*). Nevertheless, in both factories, suggestions that are accepted come significantly more often from management than from non-management council members.

From personal observation of some sessions, it was evident that, in both factories, management, and especially the director, formulated many proposals which the workers' council readily approved. The minutes of Factory B's council meetings did not disclose any instance of the rejection of a suggestion made by the director. According to Factory A's records, the workers' council

TABLE 5 *Frequency of Participation and Accepted Suggestions ·
at the Managing Board Sessions*
(Factories A and B)

| | FACTORY A | | | FACTORY B | | |
| | *33 sessions*
27/4/58 to 23/4/59 | | | *36 sessions*
27/4/58 to 29/5/59 | | |
	Manage- ment personnel	Non- manage- ment personnel	Others	Manage- ment personnel	Non- manage- ment personnel	Others
Verbal participation	150	54		84	23	
				21 sessions *19/1/59 to 22/7/59*		
Accepted suggestions	38	10	6	29	0	48
Suggestions rejected or undecided	3	0		3	0	

Note: Owing to certain difficulties in obtaining the data for Factory B, the figures presented refer to two different periods of time. This inconsistency is unlikely, however, to affect the relative proportions of management and non-management personnel, which are our interest here. Much less satisfactory is the large number of decisions taken where it was not possible to determine from the records whether the original proposal came from a management or a non-management member; these have been listed under 'Others'.

had on one occasion modified the director's proposal. This was when the director suggested that 200,000 dinars should be given to the factory's labour union; the workers' council increased the amount to 500,000 dinars (minutes of 15 August 1957).[1] At

[1] The same thing happened at a meeting of Factory A's council which I attended in July 1959.

another meeting the head of the production-technical department suggested a reduction in his own salary, and this was rejected by the council (minutes of 18 February 1959). Since both the chairmen of the workers' councils told me that they consulted with their director concerning the agenda for the meetings, it is likely that a number of the accepted suggestions that were proposed by the chairmen and therefore classified under non-management personnel in *Table 4* had been originally formulated by the directors.

The dominant position of the management personnel appears even more pronounced when the minutes of the managing board sessions are analysed in the same way (see *Table 5*).

For the analysis of the subjects discussed at workers' council and managing board sessions, as recorded in the minutes, the unit was a theme, regardless of whether it was expressed briefly or at length. The wide variety of topics was reduced to three categories, namely: production-financial; organization-maintenance; and individual applications.[2] They are best described by means of concrete examples.

---

[2] A content analysis of the minutes of workers' councils meetings in seven factories over a period of ten years was undertaken by Tanić (1961, p. 109). He used ten categories of contents which, if condensed to correspond to the more general categories employed here, would show that 50 per cent of the topics dealt with were in Category I; 30 per cent were in Category II; and 13 per cent were in Category III; the remaining 7 per cent concerned relations with external organizations – a subject not covered by my classification. These percentages correspond quite closely with my figures (see *Table 6*).

It may also be noted that in his analysis of trends over the period Tanić found that the frequency of meetings increased up to 1957, and then remained constant; that a greater variety of topics was handled; that questions of management and its organization, and of relations with external organizations, became increasingly important, as did concern with the education and welfare of employees. On the other hand, the immediate problems of production, the organization of the workers' council, and wage issues were matters that declined in importance. Tanić concludes that these changes in emphasis of the subjects dealt with, as well as the broadening scope of the problems, indicate that the workers' council has come of age; that its members have learned to deal with matters that transcend their immediate environment and concerns.

I. The production-financial category contains items such as: production planning; the purchase and sale of machines, as well as of goods produced by the factory; loans; analyses of expenditure; wages; premiums; marketing; etc.

II. The organizational-maintenance category includes items such as: the election of a new workers' council; Sunday working; health and accident-prevention measures; planning for the vacation; the formation of new committees; communication of information about activities of the workers' council; the construction of apartments for factory workers; turnover and absenteeism; etc.

III. The individual applications category contains: complaints by individual persons; applications for leave or scholarships; applications for salary increases submitted by particular persons; etc.

TABLE 6 *Classification of Topics handled by the Workers' Councils (Factories A and B)*

Category	FACTORY A 17 sessions 16/4/58 to 7/4/59	FACTORY B 22 sessions 24/4/57 to 9/4/58
I. Production-financial	51	139
II. Organization-maintenance	36	77
III. Individual applications	11	22

Note: The above data for Factory B are derived from a summary report in which the topics had already been classified into 17 categories by a factory clerk. These categories were therefore combined and allocated to the three major groups used in this study. In addition, I was able to undertake a content analysis of the minutes for 13 sessions that took place between 12 February and 23 July 1959. The frequency of themes in this analysis was as follows: Category I, 56; Category II, 44; and Category III, 37. These figures differ from those obtained from the summary report, but the rank order of the categories remains the same.

Table 6 shows that both workers' councils spent most of their time on the major goal of factory organization, i.e. production; less on maintenance problems; and least on matters concerning individuals. The managing boards, on the other hand, spent relatively more time on items in Category III (see *Table 7*). This finding could have been expected – that the smaller bodies, the managing boards, should deal with more personal problems than the larger workers' councils, which also met less often. Of course, individuals who were dissatisfied with a decision made by the managing board could, and sometimes did, appeal to the workers' council, the highest authority within the enterprise.

TABLE 7 *Classification of Topics handled by the Managing Boards* (*Factories A and B*)

Category	FACTORY A 33 sessions 27/4/58 to 23/4/59	FACTORY B 21 sessions 15/1/59 to 22/7/59
I. Production-financial	11	28
II. Organization-maintenance	17	23
III. Individual applications	25	44

Note: Bearing in mind the relative unreliability of my figures, I obtained comparable figures for Factory B's managing board from data given in the annual report for 1957–58. These were as follows: Category I, 40; Category II, 135; Category III, 58; and Miscellaneous, 37. Despite the differences between the two sets of figures, it is significant that both show, for the managing boards as compared with the workers' councils, a decrease in the discussion of production-financial affairs with a corresponding increase in the discussion of individual problems and of problems of general maintenance.

Because the category concerning individual complaints, problems, and requests was of particular interest, a further, more detailed, analysis of each item, in so far as it could be isolated from the written records, was undertaken (see *Table 8*).

The table shows that the demand for new apartments was more frequently heard than the demand for wage increases. Because of the great housing shortage, new accommodation was

TABLE 8 *Analysis of Individual Applications
handled by the Managing Board*
(*Factories A and B*)

	FACTORY A *33 sessions* *27/4/58 to 23/4/59*				FACTORY B *21 sessions* *15/1/59 to 22/7/59*			
	Total	App-roved	Post-poned	Re-jected	Total	App-roved	Post-poned	Re-jected
Wage increases	12	3	4	5	7	3		4
New apart-ments	32	7	15	10	37	12	19	6
Unpaid leave [a]	51	21	13	17				
Change of job	82	32	15	35	16	9	2	5
Study fellow-ship – financial help	9	5	2	2	16	9	2	5
An outside organization asking for financial help	19	3	16		1			1

Note: In *Tables 6* and *7* several individual complaints presented at one meeting would be classified as one unit if they referred to the same subject, because they were discussed as one item; in *Table 8* an attempt has been made to list each individual item. Therefore *Table 8* contains a greater number of individual cases than the more general Category III in the earlier tables.

[a] In Factory B requests for short periods of unpaid leave were addressed directly to the director and not to the managing board. Hence the lack of entries under this heading.

the most coveted item. In order to secure college-trained engineers and other highly trained personnel for its staff, a firm usually had to be able to offer living accommodation.

Requests from other organizations were usually submitted by communal services, such as the communal anti-tuberculosis service which wished to purchase new x-ray apparatus and asked local factories to contribute. It may be noted that the workers' council in Factory A did not show any great willingness to contribute to communal, welfare, or social improvement programmes organized or planned by communal and public organizations.

The workers' council, or its managing board, also served to some extent as a social agency, helping employees to solve their particular individual problems. In Factory A, for example, in addition to the requests listed in *Table 8*, there were, during the same period, fourteen requests for the use of the factory truck or of old material for private purposes (eight were approved and six were postponed for further consideration). It is no wonder, then, that the labour union, whose major function was to help workers in their private lives as well as in the development of skills necessary for their jobs, was overshadowed by the workers' council and its managing board.

The tendency for the workers' council to overlap, or even to compete with, the labour union programme is also seen in the numerous committees organized by the workers' council. On committees, only the data from Factory A are exhaustive.[1] There were eleven committees: one, the annual central inventory committee, had six sub-committees in six major departments of the enterprise. Delegates from the labour union, the youth organization, and management served on these committees, in addition to the workers' council members. There were committees on discipline, on hygiene and accident prevention, on the evaluation of workers, on wages, on economy, on productivity,

[1] Factory B had five standing committees and some temporary committees. Dunlop (1959, p. 292) reports that there are six standing committees of the workers' council. Our data indicate that there could be considerable differences among enterprises on this point.

on rewards, and on employment (an active and important committee, considering the great number of workers recruited by the factory during one year). The above-mentioned inventory committee, the highly skilled workers' committee, and the apartments committee were considered temporary.

The relationship between the workers' council and the commune can best be illustrated from the records of Factory B, which contained more references to the commune and the Council of Producers than did the data available for Factory A. Factory B had received some six recommendations from the Council of Producers and from the commune in which it was situated. One recommendation advised the introduction of gymnastic exercises for workers; another, the payment of war invalids during unavoidable absences; a third outlined desirable hygienic and accident-prevention standards. All these were accepted. The commune proposed new standards for overtime work in the factory, but it was not clear from the records whether these recommendations were accepted by the workers' council. Another recommendation asking for a contribution of two million dinars to the communal food service was quite clearly rejected, because the firm had already contributed three million dinars. Though this request was signed by the City Council as well as by the Council of Producers, the workers' council had no hesitation in refusing it (minutes of the council session of 2 April 1959).

Thus the relationship was not that of a one-sided dependency. The fact that the workers' council could refuse a recommendation or request made by the commune or the Council of Producers points to a certain degree of independence. Furthermore, the large number of requests for financial help that were postponed by Factory A's workers' council (see *Table 8*) is another indication that the enterprise enjoyed some freedom, especially when one considers that several of these requests were in fact from communal agencies. There is no doubt, then, that the workers' councils could exercise power, within certain limits. Of course, whether the workers actually had the power within the councils, or whether it was mainly management which acted through the workers' councils, is another issue.

THE LABOUR UNION

Within the new socio-economic system the labour union has both lost functions and acquired new ones. Its work has been defined as being not only 'more complicated but also more general and creative'.[1] It appears that the labour union is at present seeking to define its position in relation to other organizations which operate within economic institutions, especially in relation to the dominant workers' council.[2]

The data on the functioning of the labour union in Factories A and B are presented in a similar way to the data on the workers' councils. Unfortunately, less information was available concerning the union. Moreover, in both factories the records of the union committees were kept in less orderly fashion than were the minutes and other information on the workers' councils.[3]

In 1956–57 the labour union committee in Factory B was composed of four white-collar and three blue-collar members. Concerning the turnover of members, six persons (out of thirteen) on the 1958–59 committee in Factory A had also served previously, and in Factory B in the same year four former members were on the committee of nine members. According to the labour union chairman in Factory A there were no definite rules as to how frequently an individual could serve on the union committee. (There were such rules for the workers' council.) Consequently, one person had served six times, one person five times, three persons three times, and one person twice, between 1950 and 1958.

[1] See Tito's address to the Fourth Congress of the Yugoslav Labour Unions, in *Četvrti kongres Saveza Sindikata Jugoslavije Beograd 23–26 aprila 1959 godine* (1959, p. 14).

[2] While the labour union is relatively weak within the enterprise, it is stronger on a national level. The union is reported to have 1,963,000 members (see Macura, 1961). Dunlop (1959, p. 294) reports that it employed about 400 full-time paid officials.

[3] The labour union secretaries had some difficulty in gathering the minutes together and putting them in order so that an outsider could examine them. In comparison, the minutes of the workers' council meetings were kept in excellent order in both factories.

TABLE 9 *Average Attendance of Members at Labour Union Committee and Workers' Council Meetings*

(*Factories A and B*)

FACTORY A	% members present	FACTORY B	% members present
Labour union committee (1958–59, based on 3 meetings only)	50	Labour union committee (1958, 13 meetings)	63
Workers' council (1958–59, 18 meetings)	78	Workers' council (1958–59, based on 15 meetings)	81·5

TABLE 10 *Content Analysis of the Activities of the Labour Union Committees*

(*Factories A and B*)

	FACTORY A *23 meetings* *11/3/58 to 13/4/59*	FACTORY B *16 meetings* *23/1/58 to 14/11/58*

Financial help
to individuals
	27 ⎫
	   ⎬ 42
	15 ⎭
		16 ⎫
		   ⎬ 25
		9 ⎭

Material help to individuals		

Collective visits
(cinemas, countryside, etc.)
	8 ⎫
	
	   ⎬ 33
	11 ⎪
	
	14 ⎭
		7 ⎫
		
		   ⎬ 23
		6 ⎪
		
		10 ⎭

Collective training and lectures; safety regulations and wage norms		
Ceremonial-organizational events		

Evidence for the fact that less significance was attached to the labour union than to the workers' council is revealed in a comparison of the average attendances of members at meetings of the two bodies (see *Table 9*).

A content analysis of the activities of the labour union committees was undertaken in the same way as for the workers' councils, the unit of analysis being a theme. The data are presented in *Table 10*. It will be seen that in both factories the labour union's major function appears to have been to assist individuals with their personal economic problems. In this sense the union functions as a personnel department for the factory. Under both 'financial' and 'material' help to individuals are included visits and gifts to sick persons by members of the labour union. In both factories, the total of individual cases handled was higher than the total of the group activities for which the union was responsible.

These latter activities constituted the second function of the labour union, and included all the mass events in the enterprise. The union organized, for example, ceremonial occasions in memory of the foundation of the Yugoslav Communist Party; workers' council elections; the New Year's party for the children of employees; group visits to theatres; group training and lectures; and also discussions of new wage norms.

With regard to the wages issue, the labour union committee makes recommendations to the workers' council managing board concerning wage levels.[1] For example, in Factory A on 11 March 1958, the committee proposed that a meeting ought to be organized with those workers whose earnings were below the average in the enterprise. On 31 March 1959 the committee asked the managing board to let the union see the list of wage norms so that it could evaluate whether or not the wages corresponded to the positions. In Factory B the committee discussed wage norms on 11 July 1958, and there was a further reference to the same topic in the records of the annual meeting

[1] To give the reader some indication of income distribution, *Table 11* on page 32 presents relevant data from an outline of a proposal of wage norms circulated among the workers' council members in Factory A in 1959:

of the union with the whole factory collectivity (14 November 1958), when the head of the commercial department made the following critical statement: 'The union has been successful in organizing entertainment events but less so in discussions of wage norms, and in meetings with members of the managing board and with the workers' council, at which problems of the enterprise and problems of productivity are dealt with.' Thus it is legitimate to conclude that the union, though dealing also with wage matters, was more frequently concerned with other problems than that of increasing the workers' share in the enterprise's profit. Characteristically, at the annual meeting of the collectivity in Factory B, the union committee proposed

TABLE 11 *Proposed Wage Norms*
(*Factory A*)

Workers: hourly wage	Dinars
Electricians, and other highly skilled	80–115
Assistant to foreman, and other skilled	50–70
Semi-skilled	50–55
Unskilled	40
White-collar: monthly income	
Director	43,000–45,000
Lawyer	18,000–25,000
Correspondent (one foreign language)	16,000–18,000
Telephonist	11,000

The table shows that the ratio of the highest income to the lowest income within the factory is about 5:1. It was reported to me that some women earned sometimes as little as 8,000 dinars a month, though the average monthly income for unskilled and semi-skilled workers was somewhere around 10,000–12,000 dinars. However, to this sum should be added free medical care and other free social and educational services. According to Dunlop (1959, p. 304) the non-wage compensation is higher in Yugoslavia than in any other European country. It should also be noted that the director and some of the upper executives were receiving bonuses that raised their incomes. According to some employees in Factory B, the director's income was six to seven times higher than their incomes, a difference considered by them to be quite excessive.

that a certain amount of money should be invested rather than spent on consumption.

On the other hand, the union did seek to increase the amount of money it received for union activities from the workers' council. In Factory A on 9 June 1958 the committee asked the workers' council to provide it with more funds for the buffet. In Factory B, the union received 1 per cent of the net income made by the factory, and also occasionally asked for additional sums. Through these financial arrangements the union is to some extent dependent upon the workers' council.[1] For example, on 28 May 1958, the managing board of Factory B refused to accept the half-year financial report of the labour union because of 'lack of clarity'.

Some of the areas of activity of the labour union partially overlapped those of the youth organization, which also sought to organize educational and leisure activities, not only for its own members, but occasionally for all employees. Furthermore, the youth organization was concerned with the economic, health, and educational problems of persons below the age of 24, with whom the union was likewise concerned. Thus, for example, on 8 August 1958, the Factory B union committee turned down the youth organization's request that it should be responsible for selecting the young persons to be rewarded by vacations arranged by the firm at a seaside resort.

On questions of economic assistance, the union's interests overlapped those of the managing board, which also took decisions on such matters – for example, who was to get a new apartment. Generally, employees with grievances turned directly to the managing board or the director, and rarely to the labour union committee. Probably this is an indication of the secondary and limited position, in terms of influence and power, that the union held within the enterprise.[2] For example, individual

---

[1] In 1960, 50 per cent of the labour union's programme was financed by members' dues, and 50 per cent by workers' council grants.

[2] The partial overlapping of functions among the organizations operating within the enterprise was also indicated by the fact that an organization would send representatives to meetings of the other organizations. The clearest data

employees would ask the union for financial assistance on a small scale, but not for help with regard to a conflict with a supervisor.

Finally, the greater prestige accorded to the workers' council and to the director as compared with the labour union was brought out by a questionnaire survey carried out in Factory B. Seventy-eight respondents were asked: 'Who has the greatest influence in the enterprise?' Their answers are presented in *Table 12.*

TABLE 12 *Influence within the Enterprise*
(*Factory B – 78 respondents*)

		Influence attributed to:			
	Director	*Workers' council*	*Labour union*	*League of Communists*	*Don't know*
First in influence	27	45	2	4	0
Second in influence	29	22	11	11	5
Third in influence	10	4	33	19	12

Thus reflecting upon the labour union organizations within the two factories, it is evident that the union cannot be described as a 'representative symbolic' organization of the workers in the face of management. Compared with the workers' council, the union had less social significance and lower prestige within the enterprise. Financially, the union was substantially dependent upon help granted to it by the workers' council; in Factory A,

---

were obtained for the labour union in Factory B: at 14 of the 15 sessions of the labour union, representatives from other organizations were present; the secretary of the League of Communists was the most assiduous, attending on five occasions. From the content analysis of the activities of the two labour union committees, it appears that they overlapped mainly the functions of the workers' councils.

for example, the amount that the director allotted to the union was increased by the workers' council. The interrelations of the labour union and the other organizations within the enterprise further contributed to the loss of the union's symbolic function, and its spheres of activity overlapped those of some of the other organizations.

THE YOUTH ORGANIZATION

The youth organization embraced all employees in the factories who were between 14 and 25 years of age. There were no dues and no formal membership. The purpose of the organization was to educate young people especially socio-politically, as well as to provide organized leisure opportunities for them.[1] At the time of this research the youth organization in both factories was at a low ebb. Whether this was a temporary or a more permanent crisis could not be determined because of the lack of data.

As there were no records of the activities of the group for earlier years, the only fact that could be established with regard to the turnover of personnel on the committees of the youth organization was that, in each factory, one person on the 1958 committee has served also on the committee in the previous year. Certainly, this did not suggest much continuity of membership.

A study of the minutes of the meetings of the youth organization during 1958 revealed evidence of what may be termed 'organizational sickness'. A content analysis was undertaken, applying the same method and unit of measurement, and similar categories, as in the analyses of the records of the workers' council and labour union committee meetings, and the results are presented in *Table 13*.

---

[1] Started in 1948 through the merger of a Communist and a non-Communist youth organization, the National Youth of Yugoslavia (*Narodna Omladina Jugoslavije*) had 1,386,152 members in 1960. See 'Omladina' in *Enciklopedija Leksikografskog zavoda*, Vol. 5, pp. 547–8, for further information (Zagreb, 1961).

TABLE 13 *Content Analysis of Themes at the*
Youth Organization Meetings
(Factories A and B)

Category	FACTORY A 13 meetings 30/10/58 to 16/7/59	FACTORY B 6 meetings 20/11/58 to 27/5/59
Ideological and production	7	4
Organized leisure activities	8	4
Organizational	13	6

In both factories there appears to have been a tendency for the members to spend most of their time discussing organizational problems. Questions such as 'Why does the youth organization not work adequately?' were frequently raised. Despite the fact that a programme had been outlined, a later review of progress disclosed that it had not been implemented. Consequently, since so much time was taken up on these matters, less was spent on the achievement of the organization's goals. Such a situation is indicative of a kind of 'sickness'.

Further evidence on the malfunctioning of the youth organization in both enterprises is provided by a more detailed examination of the records of certain meetings. For instance, in Factory A during the meeting of 11 March 1959, it was stated that since October of the previous year no single ideological-political programme had been organized; and at the meeting on 3 May 1959 all the discussion was focused on the problem of the youth organization's failure to stimulate interest in socio-political activities among the young people in the factory. In Factory B on 26 December 1958 the meeting was devoted to a discussion of whether or not the young people had negative attitudes towards work and the enterprise. Both factories had arranged a meeting at which a lecture on the history of the Yugoslav Communist movement was given; it was recorded that 'no discussion followed the lecture'.

As far as relations with other organizations are concerned, the minutes referred most frequently to the League of Communists. On the question of the participation of youth organization members on the workers' council, figures were available only for Factory A: eighteen young persons served on the council, and three on the managing board. The chairman of the youth organization in Factory B was also a member of the workers' council in the factory. Both youth organization committees were visited by representatives of the communal or republican youth organization committees, who discussed the situation and sought to help and encourage the local organizations to increase their output of 'activities'.

THE LEAGUE OF COMMUNISTS[1]

Evidence about the activities of the Communist organization in the two factories has been gathered from the records of the other organizations. The local factory organizations of the League were involved in every kind of activity, and exercised their influence on other bodies in direct and indirect ways: directly, by sending delegates, usually the secretary of the League, to relevant meetings; indirectly, through their own members. For example, a woman in the personnel department in Factory B was a member of the workers' council as well as an active member of the League's committee in the factory. In Factory A, the head of the machine maintenance sector was a member of the League's factory committee, and of the managerial collegium and the workers' council.

The League's committees not only sent delegates to meetings of other organizations, but also themselves organized meetings. For example, the labour union committee in Factory B was summoned to a meeting with the secretary of the League organization on 18 May 1959. The secretary, accompanied by there other League members, sought to discover why the labour union had not done a satisfactory job, and why more people were not members of the union. It may be noted that the secretary stated: 'Part of the responsibility for the situation rests also upon

---

[1] The League had 830,000 members in 1959–60 (Macura, 1961, p. 431).

the shoulders of the League of Communists members. The Communists have to be propagators of the union's job. On the other hand, the union really ought to tackle problems of the enterprise, and not merely worry as to how to collect union dues.'

In Factory A, at a meeting on 24 March 1958 when the list of candidates for the next workers' council was prepared, the League's committee members participated along with representatives of the workers' council, the labour union, and the youth organization. All the ceremonial, annual sessions of the collectivity were attended by the League's representatives, who used the opportunity to comment on and evaluate the activities of the other organizations. Thus the League passed judgement upon the other bodies, but the latter did not comment upon the work of the League's factory organization which, of course, was evaluated by higher League levels within the commune, the state, and the federation.

Though the League provided a sort of authorization for the activities of the other organizations, the majority of the respondents in our sample in Factory B did not consider that it was the most influential authority within the enterprise (see *Table 12*). Another indication of the somewhat changing role of the League of Communists within the industrial organization is provided by the fact that the position of secretary to the League was no longer a paid job. In Factory A, the unpaid secretary of the League was a woman who did not give the impression of being a very influential person. In Factory B the secretary was a graduate engineer. On the other hand, it should not be forgotten that the majority of the top executives in both factories were League members. Factory B appeared to be less concerned with politics than Factory A, and this difference was probably the result of the difference in personality of the two directors.

DIFFERENCES IN ATTITUDE BETWEEN MANAGEMENT AND NON-MANAGEMENT PERSONNEL

Our discussion thus far has considered the organizations that functioned within the two factories. The management – that is, the ten persons (including the director) of the collegium in Factory A, and the less conspicuous seven persons in Factory B – constituted an informal group in each factory. My former research in Poland had led me to assume that in Yugoslavia also significant differences in attitude could be expected as between management and the other employees. Two Yugoslav research reports touched upon these differences. Sinadinović (1959), reporting on Jovan Vejnović's survey of 630 workers in Belgrade factories, stated that there appeared 'a certain number of workers who did not show interest in workers' management' (p. 151).[1] Radosavljević (1961) presented the results of a survey of 1,100 employees in four enterprises in the Republic of Serbia in 1959. It was found that both members of the workers' council and non-members tended to answer some questions according to their position within the enterprise; those who were closer to the top expressed a greater satisfaction with their pay than those who were in lower (and also less well-paid) positions (op. cit. p. 74).

My own questionnaire survey data indicate that attitudes towards the distribution or investment of profits are most characteristic on this point. Responses to the question, 'How many people think that profits should be distributed rather than invested?' are shown in *Table 14*.

TABLE 14 *Estimated Numbers in Favour of Distribution of Profits*
(Factory B – 78 respondents)

	Employees thought to favour distribution of profits:		
Respondents	*All*	*Half*	*A few*
Unskilled and semi-skilled	9	7	8
Skilled and white-collar	10	5	28
Executives[a]	1	1	9

[a] Included university graduates as well as the 7 top executives. $\chi^2 < .05$

[1] Unfortunately no more specific information was provided.

As the difference in the responses seemed especially pronounced between the unskilled and semi-skilled on the one hand, and the executives on the other, *Table 15* gives the answers of 35 respondents to a question concerning the failure of adequate communication: 'Whose fault is it that people don't always know what has been decided by the workers' council?'

TABLE 15 *Failure of Communication of Workers' Council Decisions*
(Factory B – 35 respondents)

Respondents	Responsibility for failure of communication of workers' council decisions attributed to:		
	Workers	Workers' council	Other or no answer
Unskilled and semi-skilled	4	18	2
Executives	9	1	1

$$\chi^2 < .05$$

Management and non-management personnel also differed in their answers to a question asking what ought to be done in order to make individuals feel more strongly that the factory was their property (*Table 16*).

TABLE 16 *How to Strengthen Feeling of Ownership*
(Factory B – 35 respondents)

Respondents	Suggested measures:		
	Increase education	Increase pay and rewards	Other or no answer
Unskilled and semi-skilled	2	16	6
Executives	5	3	3

$$\chi^2 < .05$$

The above data seem to support the thesis that the differences in attitude between management and non-management personnel are due primarily to the division of labour rather than to any other factor. Further evidence of the importance of position within the organization in determining attitudes towards collective ownership is shown in *Table 17*, which gives the responses of the total sample to the question: 'How many employees feel that the factory is their property?'

TABLE 17 *Estimated Numbers who Feel Sense of Ownership*
(*Factory B – 78 respondents*)

Respondents	*Employees thought to feel sense of ownership:*	
	All or many	*Half or a few*
Unskilled and semi-skilled	12	12
Skilled and white-collar	31	12
Executives	9	2

Although the differences in response between the three occupational levels are not statistically significant, the trend from the lower skilled toward the executive level is evident. The pretesting of this item had been felt to have 'political implications', in that the respondent was asked to disclose his own attitude towards collective ownership. The form of the question was therefore changed so that respondents had to give only their opinion of the attitudes of other people in the enterprise. Even so, the answers obtained were probably still distorted to some degree because of the tendency of respondents to protect themselves.

However, the other cross-sectional data presented earlier indicate the existence of differences between management and non-management personnel on several dimensions. And these differences were found in both factories, even though it was noted that in Factory B there appeared a comparatively greater degree of participation in discussions on the part of the rank-and-file workers. On the whole, functionally the power rested with management.

This conclusion is corroborated by evidence derived from meetings that I attended in both factories, and from informal contacts of various kinds, as reported in the next chapter.

POSTSCRIPT

After this book went to press, I found in A. Sturmthal's *Workers' Councils: a Study of Workplace Organization on both Sides of the Iron Curtain* (1964) a reference to Yugoslav statistical data for the year 1956,[1] which indicate that, at that time, over the country as a whole one-quarter of workers' council members were white-collar workers and one-half skilled workers. On that criterion Factory B would deviate more from the national average than Factory A. Also, Factory B was exceptional in having a female director because less than 1 per cent of all enterprises had a woman as director. As far as elections to the councils are concerned, an average of 98 per cent of employees voted, but only 2 per cent of those elected had been put forward as candidates on non-union lists (cf. p. 7 above). In this respect both the factories studied conformed to the national pattern.

[1] Federal Statistical Office, *Workers' Councils and Managing Boards of Economic Enterprises in 1956*. Statistical Bulletin No. 77 (English version).

THREE

Observations

This chapter presents data gathered from observation at meetings, and from informal conversations with employees, during my period of field work in the two factories. The period of observation in Factory A was from 25 June to 28 July 1959; however I returned to the factory occasionally in August to attend scheduled meetings of the workers' council. Altogether, I went to eleven meetings in Factory A, most of them of the workers' council or its managing board:

1A	8 July	Meeting of the management
2A	13 July	Meeting of the youth organization committee with the League's committee
3A	14 July	Meeting of the labour union with the collectivity of workers
4A	15 July	Meeting of the managing board of the workers' council
5A	17 July	Meeting of the workers' council
6A	26 July	Meeting of the managing board of the workers council with the management
7A	28 July	Meeting of the workers' council, and the continuation of the same meeting on 29 July
8A	4 August	The labour union organized meeting of the whole working collectivity
9A	6 August	Meeting of the managing board of the workers' council
10A	7 August	Meeting of the managing board of the workers' council
11A	7 August	Meeting of the workers' council

In addition to meetings, I succeeded in establishing some useful, though fleeting, contacts with several rank-and-file workers and with foremen directly in the shops.

My field work in Factory B started on 30 July and ended on 29 August. Here I succeeded in attending six meetings:

1B	30 July	Meeting of the workers' council
2B	31 July	Meeting of the labour union with the collectivity of workers
3B	18 August	Meeting of the workers' council, adjourned to 21 August
4B	24 August	Another meeting of the workers' council
5B	26 August	Meeting of the managing board of the workers' council
6B	26 August	Meeting of the committee of the labour union

I was also able to administer the questionnaire.

I observed the following criterion in selecting the material for inclusion in this chapter: that it should refer only to matters on which there was no conflict of evidence; that is to say, if the evidence from certain observed incidents was contradicted by other incidents, they are not reported here.

THE WORKERS' COUNCIL AND ITS MANAGING BOARD

The analysis of data presented in the previous chapter concerning the workers' council and its managing board showed that the part played by workers in affairs of management was relatively minor compared with that of managerial personnel. The same disproportionate participation is indicated in an overwhelming degree by the material presented below, which describes two meetings in Factory A and two in Factory B. The meetings are reported almost exactly as they were originally recorded, in order to reduce any tendency to select and emphasize points in support of the thesis of differential participation.

Meeting of the managing board of the workers' council (4A)

The meeting was held in the afternoon, in the room adjoining the director's office. Ten persons were present. There was a period of waiting for the director, and then the chairman, a foreman from the spinning shop, opened the session by taking up the agenda, which consisted of two points: first, the question of annual vacations, and second, applications and complaints.

When the second item on the agenda was being dealt with, members of the managing board, the majority of whom were from production, participated quite actively. They knew particular persons and discussed their requests. Mostly, applicants were asking for extra leave without pay, or for scholarships in order to prepare themselves for examinations. It should be pointed out that the factory offered several scholarships to enable its employees to go to evening classes or to take time off to study for examinations.

The meeting was quite informal. The chairman of the board and the other workers spoke mostly when personal problems were brought up. When managerial issues were under discussion, the director spoke most of the time. The only person who argued with him to any extent was another member of the managerial collegium who was also a member of the board, the head of the technical bureau.

Meeting of the workers' council (5A)

This meeting was held in a large room in the accounts office, where more than fifty persons could be easily seated. It was attended by thirty-seven members; thirteen were on vacation, two were sick, and one was officially on a trip outside Belgrade. All the members of the managerial collegium were present. The director did not attend.

The chairman, a floor supervisor, opened the meeting by reading the agenda, which was as follows: (i) production plan for 1960; (ii) balance sheet for the first half of 1959; (iii) regulations concerning premium payments; (iv) allocation of apartments; (v) miscellaneous. He presented the five points skilfully, and throughout the meeting kept the agenda moving, like an efficient parliamentarian.[1] He seemed to be popular.[2]

The head of the production-technical department gave a ten-minute speech outlining the production plan for 1960. Though the previous plan appeared to be only 80 per cent completed, the new plan expected the total volume of production to increase by 8 per cent, as compared with the current plan. The head's talk included a lot of figures and percentages, but none of the members took down any notes. I got the impression that people did not digest all the figures that were thrown at them. However, there were several questions when he had finished his presentation of the plan. A woman asked: 'If the plan is enlarged, will we be able to get enough raw material?' A man asked: 'How will the holiday rota be organized?' Another woman asserted that women with children could not work on the night shift which was being planned for the spinning department. These questions were dealt with by other members of the managerial collegium. It was also stated by the managerial group that for the next few years the purchase of new machines could be planned only for the spinning shop.

The third item on the agenda, the introduction of new rules concerning premium payments, elicited a lively reaction. The head of the personnel department opened the discussion by asking members whether or not they had read the outline he had sent them two weeks prior to the meeting. One person complained that he had not had time to look it over. An older man rose to his feet and said that he was against the whole idea of premium payments because the workers did not like them; furthermore, he asked why white-collar employees got more

[1] Seymour Melman, in an unpublished paper, reports that when he attended a labour union meeting at a factory during his visit to Yugoslavia in 1959, he had the feeling that possibly the participants had had virtually no experience in operating a decision-making organization. In our case, however, the chairmen of the councils in Factories A and B had been industrial workers before the second world war, and were efficient in conducting meetings.

[2] He wore a blue collar and a short coat, as the other workers did. The managerial personnel were dressed differently, in white shirts, with or without ties.

pay than workers. Another man joined him in his criticism of the premium system. The personnel officer did not accept these views: he said that everybody was paid for what he did. The question at issue was not whether to have a bonus system, but whether the proposed new regulations were satisfactory. There were two further comments by workers and two by other management persons. The young and self-assured head of the production-technical department took the floor and brought the discussion to an end by stating that premium systems were found in both capitalist and socialist societies, that they were necessary in order to maintain quality, and that perhaps there should be a group quality bonus because in the preceding year some products had been returned to the factory on account of their poor quality. It was therefore agreed to set up a committee composed of four specialists to work out further details of the premium system.

The next point on the agenda evoked the most dramatic response. During the discussion on the allocation of accommodation in the new factory-built and -owned apartment house, I noticed that some members of the council took down notes for the first time, and that they really argued the proposals that were put forward.[1] The apartments committee itself had assigned thirty-three units, and had left five to be assigned by the workers' council; a further two were reserved for the director's decision.[2]

The first to raise his voice was the lawyer:[3] 'Why was my

[1] The same happened in Factory B. There, even the proposed distribution of apartments was voted down, and a new allocation had to be undertaken (minutes of workers' council meeting 22 and 23 July 1959).

[2] As has already been mentioned, the enterprise had to be able to offer accommodation when it was competing for specialist staff in a free labour market.

[3] The enterprise had its own lawyer and two physicians. They were not members of the managerial collegium. However, the lawyer was supposed to attend meetings of the workers' council so that legal advice was available if required. I was later informed that he had been expelled from the League of Communists because he belonged to those who supported Stalin rather than Tito. However, he was presumably doing his best to be accepted again. The lawyer often tried to engage me publicly in debate concerning my political views.

name dropped from the original list that was previously approved by the workers' council?' The controller, in his role of chairman of the apartments committee, answered that the committee had not been clear about the lawyer's general situation. He was scheduled to get an apartment when the next construction project was completed. Immediately, two other men rose and asked why they had not been considered by the committee. Neither of them was a member of the workers' council. They stood behind the members,[1] who were seated. The head of personnel, who was also on the apartments committee, said that preference had been given according to seniority – whereupon another employee blurted out, 'But I have been working here for forty years'. The controller told him that his position would be considered later; but the worker, a bricklayer employed by the firm, was not satisfied, and kept protesting. At this, a foreman from the weaving shop, who was a council member, said: 'If the bricklayer doesn't get an apartment, I am giving up mine. I don't want it.'

Another council member joined in, expressing surprise that the lawyer, and a woman with a child who had to pay a high rent, should have been by-passed. How did it come about that another woman (a member of the League of Communists and a former chairman of the workers' council) who was single had got an apartment? The controller: 'Well, we have to look at the person as a human being.' The member: 'This means that the mother with a child is not a human being?' The audience laughed.

The meeting became noisier, and the chairman banged his gavel to keep order as he put the matter to the vote. He reminded the meeting that there were 260 applications for forty apartments; thus of necessity some people would have to wait for the next opportunity. There were thirty-two persons in favour of the proposed allocation, one against, and four abstentions.

The first matter under the 'miscellaneous' heading involved

[1] Meetings of the workers' council are open to all employees (see Kovač and Miljević, 1958, p. 94).

the council's approval for five people to go to Germany to purchase new machinery for the spinning shop; the second was a
request for an increase in salary by the head of the personnel
department. While this latter point was being discussed, the
personnel officer left the room. The chairman of the managing
board explained that the head of the personnel department had
responsibilities which equalled those of the head of the weaving
shop, and yet his salary was 5,000 dinars less, or 30,000 dinars at
the time. How much more should he get? One voice suggested
that he should have 34,000, another proposed 33,000. The
workers' council voted a 3,000 rise, and the personnel officer
returned to the meeting.

Another four applications were handled rather more quickly
by the council. It was also decided that fifty-six litres of milk
(12·3 gallons) should be supplied daily for those whose work involved them in unhealthy conditions; and that a worker who
did not give truthful information to the disciplinary committee
and who appealed to the workers' council should not be punished
financially (the managing board and the disciplinary committee
had suggested a 10 per cent cut in pay) but only sternly repri-
manded. Finally, because of the lack of further, more detailed,
information, an application for financial help addressed to the
enterprise by the communal anti-tuberculosis service was
adjourned to the following meeting.

Oral exchanges at the meeting were spontaneous. However,
the most lively participation occurred, as was to be expected,
when a highly personal question was being discussed – the allocation of apartments. It was at this point that some of the council
members started to make notes, whereas when the production
figures were presented (which hardly anyone could expect to
remember without notes), no one cared to jot anything down.
In general, all the suggestions put forward by the managerial
collegium were accepted, despite the fact that the elderly worker
from the finishing department voiced workers' objections concerning premium payments. There was strong moral feeling
when a single woman with a good political record got an apartment at the expense of a woman with a child. Nevertheless, a

49

large majority voted approval of the apartment allocation policy.

Meeting of the workers' council (4B)
At this meeting I took a frequency count of members' participation. The total participation score was 104: of this, the director had the highest score, having spoken 32 times; the workers' council chairman scored 20; and the chairman of the managing board 12. Of the twenty-four persons who attended the meeting, eleven were from the managerial and white-collar groups. Not all of those present spoke at this session, but most of the managerial and white-collar employees did so. Taken together, these two groups scored 88 of the total participation score of 104; that is, they took the floor approximately 80 per cent of the time, compared with the blue-collar council members who were responsible for the remaining 20 per cent – a ratio that indicates the dominance of the director and the managerial personnel.

Meeting of the managing board of the workers' council (5B)
This meeting lasted about four hours, from about 7 a.m. to a little after 11. In addition to the personnel officer and the assistant director, seven members of the managing board were present, and the director himself dropped in twice for a few minutes. Furthermore, at one stage the managing board summoned a production unit supervisor to explain a particular point relating to one of the workers under his supervision.

The whole meeting was spent in analysing individual complaints and requests. Most of the requests were for a rise in pay, and were based on comparisons with other salaries in the shop concerned; applications were accompanied by written evaluations prepared by the relevant supervisors. Since each applicant was usually known personally by some members of the managing board, general participation was high. Individuals took the floor a total of 295 times: the chairman spoke most frequently, 92 times; the assistant director scored 73; the chairman of the labour union, 43; and the members of the managing board scored from 33 to 12. In sum, the managerial personnel contributed approximately two-thirds of the remarks, and the workers one-third. Thus the workers took the floor at this session of the managing board half as often again as the worker members at the council meeting described above. Doubtless the personnel problems lent themselves better to workers' participation than the more remote and less familiar problems of finance, technology, and marketing.

An interesting difference of opinion was revealed between the personnel officer and the assistant director on the one hand, and the worker members of the board on the other. On two occasions the management representatives favoured a rise for an older person, despite the fact that his productivity was no greater than hitherto; two worker members opposed the increase on the ground that the criterion of age should not be considered. The chairman of the labour union did not take a stand on this issue. Furthermore, the same two worker members opposed a rise for fellow workers who had failed to pass an examination for skill; the personnel officer again showed a more lenient attitude by pointing out that the examination was too rigorous for semi-skilled workers.

Here I would draw attention to three points concerning the four meetings described above. First, at Factory A workers' council meeting (5A), workers' opposition (whether it was desirable or not) was not organized, and therefore it petered out. At the meeting of the managing board in Factory B (5B) the labour union chairman who attended the meeting did not in fact defend some workers' requests for a rise, whereas management did.

Second, in all the four meetings there was plenty of opportunity for individual members to air their opinions. When they were sufficiently motivated, workers did not fail to make use of the chance to speak out, but they did not play a large part in deciding issues which were of keen concern to management because they were not particularly interested in these matters. Provided that members of the workers' council did not lose direct contact with other workers, the council served as a good channel of communication between workers and management.

Third, the fact that a top management person's salary was publicly discussed could contribute to the establishment of 'public control' over management. The analytical data did not bring out this publicity function of the workers' council. In general, the council functioned as a small internal parliament of the enterprise. But it was a special kind of parliament, as will be discussed in the final chapter.

THE LABOUR UNION

Meeting of the labour union with the collectivity (3A)

At 2 p.m. when the morning shift was leaving the factory, a meeting of the labour union was held in the great assembly hall of the administration building. The director stood at the factory gate and sought to induce people to attend the meeting, saying: 'Where are you hurrying to? Why don't you go to the meeting?' A woman argued that she would miss her train: 'Never mind,' said the director, 'go to the assembly hall.' To another worker he said: 'This is your meeting; you must go.'

Among the six persons sitting behind the desk at the front of the hall was the chairman of the youth organization.[1] The labour union chairman, a single woman in her late thirties, opened the meeting. There were three items on the agenda: first, to review the activities of the labour union for the recent period; second, to discuss the ways by which the workers' council familiarized workers with its decisions; and third, to consider the problem of the quality of production. One of the first points brought out was that members of the labour union committee were rarely seen in the factory shops. The union chairman retorted that the workers in general were little interested in the union's activities, that they became interested only when their personal problems were involved. A woman from the audience complained that the

[1] It was the policy to encourage members of the youth organization to participate in activities of other organizations within the factory. Nineteen members of the youth organization were on the workers' council.

workers' council rarely informed workers about its policies. Presumably the bulletin board in her department was empty. Another person asked which would be preferable: to have oral information about the workers' council's activities or a written announcement posted on the board. The union chairman answered that both channels ought to be used.

The subject of the quality of production did not create any response at the beginning. Several persons at the back of the assembly room were leaving. The speaker, the quality controller, again appealed for comments.[1] A young worker, though he had been in the factory only a short time, felt compelled to say that in his previous place of employment the workers were more involved. In his view, the labour union here – with the exception of the woman chairman – was not working well. He appealed to his fellow workers to identify themselves with their responsibilities in the factory. In conclusion, the secretary of the factory organization of the League of Communists, also a woman in her thirties,[2] said: 'Today's meeting is not satisfactory. People have come here without any preparation. First, we must organize meetings in particular departments with smaller numbers of workers, so that each worker can compare himself with his fellow workers. It is absolutely necessary to arrange things differently next time.'

The major problem that kept cropping up was how to motivate workers to participate more fully in factory affairs, to identify themselves with the enterprise.

Meeting of the labour union committee (6B)
This was the only labour union committee meeting I was able to

---

[1] The quality controller, whose position in the factory was new, was directly responsible to the director. The controller was a man in his thirties, a highly skilled foreman who had trained in evening courses, and kept rising in the hierarchy of the factory organization. It should also be noted that the year before he had been secretary of the factory organization of the League of Communists.

[2] This woman was married and had a gymnasium education, which is approximately the equivalent of junior college or sixth-form grammar school.

attend. In the small assembly hall where both the workers' council and its managing board had met before, a group of five persons talked in animated fashion for an hour and a half one afternoon. Towards the end of the meeting the secretary of the League of Communists appeared. Of the five members of the committee, three were white-collar persons and two manual workers. In terms of participation, the white-collar employees again dominated the discussions: of the total verbal participation score of 221, the three white-collar committee members spoke 190 times, and the two workers only 31 times.

The first subject of discussion was the labour union budget. The union had obtained money from the workers' council, but at the time of the meeting was in the red. It was suggested that, at the next social function the union organized, the sale of beer might provide additional income. Another possible source of income might be the sale of rejects. The committee approved the purchase of weight-lifting apparatus for the gymnasium at a cost of 40,000 dinars. Other items to be purchased were a television set and a radio receiver for the use of employees.

A point that throws light on the relationship between the labour union and other organizations was raised by the head of the accounts office. The chairman of the union committee wanted one of its members to sit as a delegate on the committee responsible for the distribution of new apartments; but the accountant wanted an apartments committee composed entirely of labour union members.[1] He said: 'We are struggling to increase our reputation among the workers. The question is whether the labour union organization means anything in the enterprise. We should have our own apartments committee, and in addition we should send a delegate to the workers' council committee.' The chairman replied: 'How can we have our own committee? We haven't any apartments.' The accountant said: 'But we can still express our opinions.'

Generally, there was much disagreement among the three white-collar members. Nevertheless, no votes were taken on any

[1] A proportion of the profits made by Factory B was used – as in Factory A – for the construction of factory-owned apartment houses.

issue. The topics discussed manifested the social welfare function of the union within the enterprise. Concern about the union's loss of influence was clearly voiced by the head of the accounts office.

The two labour union meetings described require little further comment. The observations support the evidence presented in the previous chapter. The union was not only struggling to gain a new status but was also seeking to define its role: should it become a part of management – a sort of personnel department – or should it play a more autonomous role in regard to management? Because it was financially dependent to some extent upon the workers' council and upon management, the labour union's striving towards autonomy was of course hampered.

THE YOUTH ORGANIZATION AND THE LEAGUE OF COMMUNISTS

Meeting of the youth organization committee with the League's committee (2A)

Another organization struggling not so much with the definition of its role as with the apathy of its members was the youth organization. The above meeting of the youth organization committee and the League of Communists committee was the only meeting of each of these organizations that I was able to attend.[1]

At the beginning, the chairman of the youth organization (who had attended the labour union meeting (3A) described above) admitted that, over the recent period, the organization had had more difficulties than successes in its work. Therefore the committee was meeting with the League of Communists committee to seek advice and help.

The head of the machine maintenance shop,[2] who participated

[1] I had some difficulty in obtaining information concerning membership of the League. Later, the director frankly asked me not to seek this information. Consequently, I did not pursue the matter further, though my assistant assured me that membership of the League – contrary to former practice – was public at that time.

[2] He was a university graduate, and at the time was also a member of the Federal Council of Producers.

in the meeting as a League member, started a long analysis of the failures of the youth organization. He said that individualism, lack of discipline, and anarchism had again appeared. Young people must become aware of the new social reality in which they were all living, and of the advantages of the socialist system; they must realize that Yugoslavia was today struggling for a higher standard of living.

When he had finished speaking, there was some discussion of other reasons for the failure of the youth organization. One young person commented that young people chose to go directly to the labour union for help instead of coming to the youth organization. Another complained that some sports equipment was not available, a point contested by the personnel officer. Finally, the director spoke in his straightforward way: 'The youth organization committee has not worked as hard as is necessary. I do not know how you waste your time. I have not seen or heard of one single meeting of the Young Producers' Club.[1] And yet so many opportunities are open to you. When we were fighting, everything was considerably more difficult. Of course, I do not want to return to those conditions. But it is up to you. We are not going to take this factory with us to the grave; it is yours.' The director also made some caustic comments on how some of the young women dressed themselves, coloured their hair, smoked, and tended to spend all their free time on the river bank. Representatives of the youth organization protested. They said that the picture was not as black as the director had suggested; they affirmed that they were motivated to work.

As well as illustrating some of the youth organization's problems (which were similar in Factory B), this meeting brings out the 'moral authority' role of the League's organization within the factory.

---

[1] This was a special sub-organization where technological problems and innovations were supposed to be discussed. Its purpose was to encourage interest in the production and technological training of workers.

DIFFERENCES BETWEEN MANAGEMENT AND WORKERS

Apathy and lack of interest in organizational activities and managerial problems did not plague only the youth organization; they also characterized to a greater or lesser degree the mass of employees in both factories. The following data are from Factory A, where I was able to get to know several men and women in different shops before the director intervened in the research. Again, attitudes expressed in interviews and conversation revealed differences in outlook between workers and management.

Interview with time-study assistant
This was the first interview I had in Factory A with a highly communicative respondent; her job title was 'time-study assistant'. She reported a conflict she had had with her former immediate supervisor. She had thought that she was entitled to get two dinars per hour more than she had received at first. In order to get the prescribed amount, she had complained about the head of the weaving shop to the head of the production-technical department; and she had got her money. 'And how about the labour union?' I asked. 'It's no use going to the union,' she answered, 'it is better to see the director himself.'

Her description of her own job was very interesting. She said that the workers did not like what she did, so she did not tell them which machine she was observing while walking around with her stop-watch. She stated that she could see when a worker was slowing down merely by watching. 'What do you do when you see someone going slow?' I asked her. 'Well, I tell the worker that I am aware of it and that he or she should start working at the normal rate.'

First survey concerning knowledge of the activities of the workers' council
In anticipation of this survey, a few days before the workers' council meeting that I attended (5A, see p. 45 above), I tried to get to know particular workers in different shops by talking to them about their work and telling them about myself. Then, the

day after the meeting, I went to see the same persons again to find out whether they knew anything about the meeting. I started this survey after the fifteen-minute morning break during which employees could walk around and talk.

I talked to twenty-four people who were employed in the weaving, spinning, repair, and maintenance shops. They worked near members of the current workers' council, most of whom I had seen the day before at the meeting. Consequently, they could have been expected to learn something about the agenda of the meeting from the council members.

Of the twenty-four individuals with whom I spoke that morning, ten did not know anything about the meeting; eleven knew about the allocation of apartments; one knew that premium payments had been discussed; and one person knew that the personnel officer had got a rise, which was, in his opinion, undeserved because it was ten times higher than his own rise. Surprisingly, a foreman who had served as chairman of the second workers' council[1] did not know anything of the meeting. Somewhat apologetically he said: 'It is not the practice to report the workers' council agenda to workers. However, there will be a meeting of the council with the whole collectivity present, when the mid-year balance sheet will be presented.'

Some people who knew how the apartments had been distributed expressed their dissatisfaction, claiming that only Party members or white-collar workers were rewarded. One person, who could be described as a floor supervisor and who had talked to me earlier in Marxist terms, stated in a sudden blunt outburst: 'Only white-collar workers get apartments; we workers do not get anything.'

Second survey concerning knowledge of the activities of the workers' council

While the director was out of town, the personnel officer gave me permission to go about in the factory once more. I went back to the spinning shop to see my 'old friends' among the women

---

[1] Each year since 1950 a new workers' council has been elected. People identified the councils by ordinal numbers.

who worked there. First, I talked to the two women who served on the workers' council. They told me about the council meeting on 7 August (11A, see p. 61 below) and said that they had not known beforehand that it had been arranged to purchase a machine for their shop, and that this would be proposed by the shop's foreman at the council meeting. The foreman – who was also chairman of the managing board – told me that he had discussed the matter with the manager of the shop and with one other man, an articulate member of the workers' council, but he had not mentioned the decision to buy a new, expensive machine to anyone else in the spinning shop.

When I was in the shop I noticed a bulletin concerning the labour union meeting with the collectivity, held on 4 August (8A).[1] It had been hung so high that most of the women could not have read it; as a matter of fact, they did not even look at the notice board. The same bulletin was also posted on another board in the spinning shop, but in an equally inaccessible position. Obviously those persons who, following the director's appeal, put the notices up, took it for granted that nobody would read them anyhow.

In the maintenance shop I asked a foreman which of the three major shops – spinning, weaving, and finishing – fell furthest below its target for the fulfilment of the plan. He gave the correct answer – the weaving shop – and I asked him where he got his information: 'From the labour union meeting,' he answered. Another worker, however, was unable to answer the same question. When I asked him whether he had read the notice which listed the percentages of the plan that had been completed, he replied rather scornfully that he did not care to read it. In another part of the spinning shop, and in the weaving and finishing shops, I asked seven women at random the same question about which department was furthest behind on the plan. They did not know, and had not read the bulletin. One of them explained apologetically: 'We have children; this is of no interest to us.' However, there was one woman who knew the

---

[1] As a result of my findings in the first survey, the director had asked (at 8A) for bulletins of meetings to be posted up.

correct answer, and she said that she had heard the director give it at the labour union meeting.

I met the chairman of the workers' council walking with the controller, and I told them how my questions had been answered. The controller said: 'Those who are interested know.' 'But the majority do not seem to be interested,' I said. The controller smiled and explained: 'Well, they are always interested when they think that their pay packets are directly involved, otherwise not.' It appears that the controller put his finger on the fact that for most of the workers the gulf between their efforts and financial rewards in the form of profit-sharing seemed too wide.

Thus the attitudes expressed by workers in Factory A in conversation and informal interviews bear out the conclusions based on the questionnaire survey in Factory B as reported in the previous chapter. Despite the fact that they participated in the sharing of profits, workers still differentiated themselves from management. The Yugoslav workers' reaction to time and motion study is encountered in many British and American factories. Likewise, their lack of interest in the agenda of the workers' council is similar to lack of interest in union meetings on the part of British and American rank-and-file union members.[1] All the evidence gathered from observations of meetings and from informal talks with employees in both factories validated the proposition that the vast majority of the workers were only lukewarm, though not antagonistic, in their attitudes towards factory organization and management, and displayed a low degree of interest in management participation.

A white-collar worker's attitude

Although white-collar personnel displayed a greater degree of interest in and knowledge about factory affairs, they did not necessarily develop a greater identification with the enterprise. The following incident is a case in point.

I happened to be with the head of the personnel department in Factory B when a young single woman, a member of the factory

[1] See Tannenbaum and Kahn (1958, p. 53).

labour union committee – and one of the best white-collar employees, according to the personnel officer – came to ask to be released from her duties. He obviously disapproved of her move and sought to induce her to stay. The girl wanted to go to a commercial establishment, where she felt she would have better opportunities. 'Well,' said the personnel officer, 'you are considering it only from your personal viewpoint and not from the viewpoint of the enterprise.' But the young woman was not convinced that she had any responsibility towards the enterprise: 'According to the law I am free to leave if I wish,' she said. Then the personnel officer argued that she would never make as much money elsewhere as she could make in the enterprise. The girl seemed unmoved, and left after a few more words. I then asked the personnel officer why employees left the factory, and he listed four reasons: (i) an opportunity to obtain a new apartment; (ii) a long journey between home and the factory; (iii) personal circumstances, such as marriage; (iv) pay.

It was reported to me that a chairman of the workers' council in Factory B had previously left for a more lucrative position elsewhere, and that white-collar employees had the highest rate of leaving. Obviously, level of aspiration, expectations of achieving a desired goal, opportunity to move, as well as knowledge about openings elsewhere, would affect all employees regardless of their positions. However, those who were in higher positions of leadership were likely to be influenced by correspondingly higher normative expectations, as the questionnaire data suggest (see *Tables 14* and *17* above).

ENTERPRISE AND COMMUNITY

Finally, two incidents are reported which touch on the relationship of the enterprise with the commune in which it was located.

Meeting of the workers' council (11A)
This meeting was held in August in the great assembly hall, although only thirty-nine persons were present owing to the absence of many employees on holiday. At the beginning, the

director delivered a speech almost an hour in length about the current financial situation of the enterprise.[1] When he had finished and the council was invited to comment, there was, surprisingly, silence. The audience was tired. So the director started to elaborate further himself, cracking a joke about the unofficial use of the factory car.[2]

Greater interest was shown, however, when regulations concerning premium payments and new wage norms came up for discussion. On the latter subject there was open disagreement between the director and the head of the technical-production bureau. The director maintained that every job in the factory would have a norm according to which job performance would be measured. The production head disagreed, arguing that some maintenance jobs could not be quantitatively evaluated.[3]

Following this unresolved disagreement, business moved rapidly. The director opposed a proposal to sell old rags to employees; he said that it was illegal. However, the chairman suggested a way whereby the labour union could buy the rags from the factory and then sell them to workers. The chairman said: 'Let the director complain to the commune; we shall do it this way.'

Another point to be noted here is that the chairman of the managing board, himself foreman of the spinning shop, proposed (and the council accepted the proposal) that a new machine be bought for the spinning department.

This meeting again provided an example of disagreement among managerial personnel. The director formally vetoed the decision of the workers' council to sell old rag material to

[1] He asked me not to note down what he was saying 'because of competition'.

[2] The director said that people ought to watch him, because the next time he found a girl friend for himself (he was a bachelor in his early fifties), he would take her for a ride in the factory car. The same sensitivity to the unofficial use of official transport was also shown by workers' council members in Factory B.

[3] At this time the factory engaged an outside team of experts to help them to develop more satisfactory norms for different jobs in the factory. I was later told that the team was not very successful and left after a few weeks.

workers because it was his legal duty to do so. However, as he did this, there was a 'joking relationship' between him and the chairman of the council; everybody understood that the director was in fact in favour of the step taken by the council.[1]

The adjourned meeting of the workers' council (3B)
Only that part of the meeting is described which is relevant to the consideration of enterprise – community relations.

After a short intermission, the director reported to the council a recommendation concerning hygienic and accident-prevention measures, which had been received from the commune's office. The secretary of the League of Communists factory organization who was present at the meeting (he was not a member of the council) spoke up for the first time. 'Despite improvements,' he said, 'one has to realize that workers do not like to use new preventive measures.' It is noteworthy that the League took the floor only on this one occasion during the meeting, and then in connection with a relatively uncontested problem.

The first of these two incidents illustrates well the degree of autonomy enjoyed by the enterprise in regard to the communal Council of Producers. And the second indicates the role of the League of Communists within the enterprise. On the basis of indirect evidence also – i.e. the scarcity of references made to the League during workers' council and other meetings – the League apparently was not a frequent initiator, but rather an observer and censor.

In general, the observational data support the evidence supplied by the analytical data. The workers' council appears again as the most vital organization within the enterprise, with the labour union and the youth organization lagging behind. The

[1] It was explained to me that the case would be taken up at community level but that no harm would come to the factory. The workers' council chairman felt that he would be able to defend his move. On another occasion the chairman told me that he always discussed the agenda with the director before the council meeting. Similar consultations between the director and the chairman were reported to me in Factory B. Obviously, then, the formal veto by the director was agreed upon prior to the meeting.

importance of the workers' council in providing a channel of communication between management and workers has been made clear from the observational data. On the other hand, evidence derived from informal contacts with the rank and file has also shown that many employees were quite uninterested in the agenda of the workers' council. The implications of these seemingly contradictory tendencies are considered in the final chapter, which also offers a theoretical interpretation of the research findings.

FOUR

Conclusion and Interpretation

In attempting to relate the analytical and observational data from the two factories I shall introduce the concept of the social system. Each factory is conceived as a more or less closed system, made up of organizations and of the collectivity of workers. Since the differences between the factories – as far as our data indicate – are not striking, in this analysis I shall concentrate upon those elements which were common to both enterprises.

The social system of the Yugoslav factory is placed within an industrial and national society with all its concomitant inter-dependencies, embodied especially in the framework of the national production plan, in financial controls exercised by federal and communal banks, and in social controls emanating from the local people's committees. It has been shown that in both factories all four organizations – management, workers' council, labour union, youth organization – and doubtless also the League of Communists organization, were engaged in inter-actions with their respective higher levels. It may be noted that, from the formal viewpoint, management was the only structure which did not have any direct supervision. When interacting with the communal or higher bodies, management operated within the framework of the workers' council. Legally, the workers' council was invested with the highest authority.

While it is true that the workers' councils and other support-ing organizations were enmeshed in the structure of social rela-tions that make up a modern industrial society, they were also searching for an organizational autonomy. Though the higher levels occasionally sent communications to the workers' coun-cils, not all their recommendations were accepted. On the other hand, the records did not disclose that the labour union or the youth organization had ever rejected any suggestions sent to them by their communal, republican, or federal bodies. On that count, then, the workers' council would appear to be the body with the greatest degree of autonomy.

Normatively, the other organizations were supposed to support the workers' council/management in their efforts to improve and increase production. In so far as this was done, the flow of functions could be represented by a circle. The mass of employees, the collectivity, is the source as well as the object of the circular process. It is the source of legitimization for the League of Communists by virtue of the fact that individual members of the collectivity are simultaneously members of the local commune, whose people's committee is the supreme organ, to which organs of the state are also subordinated.[1]

The League of Communists acts – or claims to act – on behalf of the people; it functions as a moral integrative institution. Though standing less in the foreground than in other Communist countries, the League is still the ultimate political authority. The League is not a mass organization, but unites persons who excel in some respect, especially those who display (or who ought to display) a greater political-civic awareness and responsibility. The League, then, exercises its influence upon the director (who is usually a League member) and upon the workers' council, as well as upon the labour union and the youth organization. We have seen how in Factory B the secretary of the League's factory organization attended, at least for part of the time, the meeting of the workers' council (3B) and the meeting of the labour union committee (6B). In Factory A, the League actually organized a meeting with the youth organization (2A), and the League's secretary openly criticized the labour union meeting (3A). Such action indicates that in both factories the League tended to be more often concerned with the labour union and the youth organization than with the workers' council. Two factors probably contributed to this situation: (i) in both factories the workers' council seemed to be

[1] Djordjević and Pašić (1961, p. 398).

more efficient than the labour union and the youth organization. (ii) in both factories the workers' council was under the direct influence of the director, who also was a prominent member of the League's organization. There could thus have occurred a certain informal division of labour, in the sense that the League's secretary was supposed to deal more with organizational tasks than was the director, who with his top lieutenants was primarily concerned with production and sales within the framework of the workers' council. Furthermore, the workers' councils – together with management – were more nearly autonomous bodies and had greater prestige than the labour union or youth organization. Therefore in both factories it was easier for the League's secretary to exercise influence in regard to the organizations which had less prestige and power.

The managing boards and the workers' councils worked out a reasonably good division of labour (see *Tables 4, 5, 6, 7,* and *8*). Meetings of the managing boards (4A and 5B) dealt with individual cases and prepared reports for the workers' council only if a controversy existed concerning a decision taken by the board. As the allocation of apartments was the most explosive issue in both factories, the workers' council handled it in its role of the highest authority within the enterprise (see 5A; and p. 47, note 1).

The labour union and the youth organization were supportive organizations of the workers' council. The fact that they were financially dependent upon the workers' council contributed to their secondary role (6B). They frequently transmitted initiatives originating with the workers' council to the collectivity of workers – for instance, at one union meeting with the workers (3A), an item on the agenda was the problem of the quality of products. Furthermore, the labour union, and the youth organization in the case of young people, were the only mass organizations to which everyone could belong. As a matter of fact, there was in both factories a steady mild pressure upon employees to join the union and to participate in the youth organization. But being mass organizations, with a great number of apathetic and uninterested members, these two

67

bodies were lacking in vigour (see 2A, 3A, and 6B; and *Tables 9, 10,* and *12*).

Thus the labour union and the youth organization transmit initiatives to the collectivity which, it will be remembered, endows the League with authority. This completes the theoretical circle (see *Figure 1*).

Figure 1. The Theoretical Circle

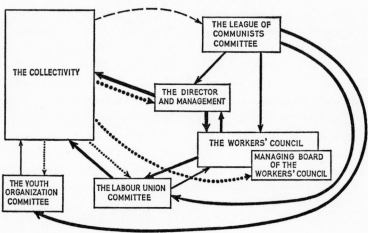

——— Signifies authorization
——— Signifies organizational influence
••••••••• Signifies individual requests
The heaviness of the rules corresponds approximately to the degree of importance or frequency of the interaction

Note: The diagram is an approximate representation of the social interaction/influence structure in Factories A and B at the time of the research. At other times and in other factories, different structures could be found.

The League's influence on management and on the workers' council is depicted as less strong than its influence on the labour union and the youth organization, in accordance with the data from both factories (see 2A and 6B). The labour union seeks to initiate some action for the workers' council but the union's influence on the council is less frequent and powerful than the council's influence upon the labour union. Individuals make some appeals to the labour union, but most of the personal applications are addressed either directly to management or to the workers' council's managing board. The diagram also shows the central position of the director and management, whose suggestions were practically always accepted by the workers' council. Through the council, management seeks to influence the labour union.

From the diagram can be seen the functional adjustments that had been made. First, the collectivity, as such, related to the four major organizations through individuals; second, the collectivity could express itself through the worker members within the workers' council and its managing board. On the other hand, the organized bodies exercised a stronger influence upon the collectivity than the collectivity exercised on them. There were three organizational structures by means of which the mass of men and women could be reached, in addition to the daily managerial contacts with workers within the production process. The workers' council and its managing board formally interacted with the collectivity through the managerial structure; management was supposed to implement the decisions of the workers' council. The other two bodies which came in contact with workers and sought to organize them were the labour union and the youth organization. All meetings with the collectivity were organized by the labour union; and the youth organization was urged to seek out young persons within the enterprise and to get them interested in organizational and socio-political issues. The youth organization's major function was to 'socialize' young persons for their future social roles within the industrial organization. Both the labour union and the youth organization were more often concerned with maintenance problems than with production; the managerial structure, of course, was predominantly occupied with production problems.

Thus, though normatively all these organizations were supposed to interact on an equal basis, the functional adjustment resulted rather in a circular flow of initiated actions, and a tendency to divide problems along the maintenance/production axis. The functioning of the whole social system results in a new division of labour, and this in turn contributes to the equilibrium

F

of the system. Heuristically considered as an isolated social system, the 'theoretical circle' could generate activities as a sort of *perpetuum mobile*. The critical link is that between the collectivity, predominantly uninterested and socially passive, and the selective and responsibility-conscious group of persons within the League's factory organization. The assumption that the League is the guardian of the basic interests of the working collectivity lies outside the scope of our inquiry here; but such an assumption relates the most responsible group to the less responsible. Since it is diffused and general, this relationship generates action. If two equally apathetic and uninterested groups come together within the organization, the result could be merely inactivity. Thus, in theory, an action within the organization that is not disruptive to it is more likely to occur when there is a certain lack of balance in the motivation of the two persons or groups.

So far, we have shown how the functional requirements of the daily operations led to certain adjustments between the organizations. But if the norm was explicitly stated, the natural functional tendency was restrained, and social processes fell closer to the norm. For example, a natural functional tendency was to select more able persons for the workers' council in both factories (*Table 1*); unskilled workers were seldom elected. And it can be assumed that, if it had not been legally prescribed that three-quarters of the managing board's members must be directly employed in the line of production, representation on the board would also have been disproportionate, in favour of the staff and highly skilled personnel. It may be noted that the proportion of skilled and semi-skilled workers on the managing boards is similar in both factories, although the two workers' councils were not similar in this respect.

Inasmuch as the norm suppresses the natural tendency to select better qualified personnel for positions of leadership, it could be concluded that, of necessity, it creates a certain stress and malfunctioning within the social system. On the other hand, in the sense that the legal norm helped to keep open channels connecting the rank and file with top management, it could be said that its effect was beneficial. After all, the management proposed the great majority of the decisions anyhow, and so the presence of relatively incompetent persons did not matter (see *Tables 4* and *5*). The legal provisions stipulated that no one could serve for three consecutive years; this also helped to keep channels open between the 'lows' and the 'highs' (*Table 3*).

Nevertheless, the communicative importance of the features here discussed should not be overemphasized. There was considerable evidence to the effect that council members, on returning to their jobs after a meeting, did conspicuously little reporting of the council's activities, and that other workers showed little interest in obtaining such information (see pp. 57–60 above). Likewise, meetings organized by the labour union at which the workers' council presented an account of its activities over the recent period did not attract interest and involvement on the part of the collectivity (8A, 2B).

It has been shown, then, that all the organizations within the factory made functional adjustments in relation to one another. At first sight the whole system appeared to be highly integrated. Further analysis disclosed, however, that groups tended to compete; moreover, individual workers manifested their dissent from time to time. In more general terms, there was a tendency to express differences resulting from the division of labour. Thus the problem was to discover whether there were differences between the workers and the managerial personnel.

Data from the questionnaire survey (*Tables 12–17*) provide evidence that the rank-and-file workers differ significantly from management. Furthermore, there was a tendency for 'organizational egoism' to appear – for example, in the 'who gets what' issue between the labour union and the youth organization in Factory B. The labour union's desire to gain greater recognition by being in charge of the allocation of new apartments (6B) indicates the same problem. The union wanted to play a somewhat more active role in regard to the workers' council and to management. In Factory A the union requested increased funds; since, however, the funds came from the workers' council and from management, the union was dependent upon these bodies. Thus the labour union could offer only a weak opposition to

71

management, and consequently it also lost its vital function of being the workers' organization (see 3A and 6B, and p. 57 above). It is reasonable to suggest, then, that if the union could have become financially independent of the managerial structure, it would have regained a place of importance.

On the other hand, as far as the workers' council is concerned, the fact that the council or its managing board worked in close cooperation with management precluded its becoming a genuine workers' body. The workers' council tended to be identified with management because of the overlap between the two bodies. This is illustrated, for example, by a statement made by a worker member of the council during a discussion on how much of the profits should be allocated to employees: 'It is necessary to divide something for 1957 among the workers, otherwise the workers will look at it differently and will say that we are not their representatives' (minutes of Factory B council meeting, 1958). Another instance was reported above – when an elderly worker at a council meeting (5A) opposed the introduction of new work norms; since he was not supported by any organization, however, his view was not even put to the vote, and the workers' council followed the policy that had the support of all the management persons present.

Incidents such as these show that the labour union had a better chance of becoming a workers' organization than the workers' council. The workers' council functioned as a parliament, where the two major production groups met. If the workers had an organization of their own, as the management has its collegium, there would be a more balanced relationship between the men who manipulate concepts and the men who manipulate things. Yugoslav theory, on the other hand, has sought rather to decrease the management-labour dichotomy.[1] The dependence of the other organizations – financially upon management and the workers' council, and morally/institutionally upon the League – is one mechanism by which this has been achieved. Another is

[1] During my stay in Factory B the personnel officer told me that Yugoslav legal publications were discontinuing the distinction between white-collar and manual workers.

the practice of overlapping membership: each of the four bodies had members who belonged also to other organizations. The only division of power expressed so far is the rule that the director cannot be simultaneously the chairman of the workers' council. Otherwise practice has moved in the direction of merging management and workers; for example, the head of the personnel department (i.e. management) was delegated to represent the labour union at the city labour union conference (minutes of Factory B labour union meeting, 11 March 1959). And the fact that the director tried to induce workers to go to a labour union meeting instead of to their homes after an eight-hour working day (see 3A, p. 52 above) would make it difficult for workers to take much interest in that organization, if they had grievances against the director.

This analysis has so far been carried out within the boundaries of the social system of the factory. It has been shown that there existed tendencies towards differentiation which were only partially channelled by existing organizations. Having pointed out the functional difficulties of the social system, let me now stress its positive aspect – especially when compared with my earlier experience in a Polish factory. In both Poland and Yugoslavia I observed differentiation between labour and management. However, hostility towards management was apparently stronger among Polish workers than in the two Yugoslav factories. Even allowing for chance factors, the difference could be explained as deriving from the greater autonomy of the Yugoslav enterprise. For the Polish workers, management and all the other higher personnel were perceived as a diffuse and generalized category, labelled 'they' (Kolaja, 1960, pp. 78–82). It was an invisible management of which the actions and motivations were not quite clear and which consequently became an easy object of suspicion and scapegoating. In the two Yugoslav factories, and especially in Factory B, complaints and hostile remarks tended to be concrete and tangible, referring to specific issues that did not lend themselves as easily to scapegoating. In the Yugoslav case there was definitely more give-and-take between management and labour. The Yugoslav workers' council system was an established institution, whereas the Polish workers' council was an experiment.

In his evaluation of the Yugoslav case, Dunlop lists seven points that result from it.[1] My field experience corroborates six of his findings, but I would elaborate upon Dunlop's fourth statement, which maintains that the workers' council contains and directs protests and dissatisfactions which inevitably arise during the process of industrialization. First, it could be asked whether the inevitable protests and dissatisfactions arise only during the process of industrialization. Are not these protests in fact the result of tensions that are likely to occur in any society that is experiencing social change – as all modern societies continually do? Second, the point about the containment and direction of protests within the workers' council may be referred to my earlier definition of the council as 'a parliament of a special nature'. This term was intended to express both the considerable opportunities for communication provided by the council and its managing board and, simultaneously, the little likelihood of the coming into being of an organized opposition. Dunlop fails to make clear that the workers' council ordinarily serves as a means for individual protest, or at most for only temporary, informally organized protest. It could, of course, be suggested that because the protest issues are local issues there is no need for any particular organization, and therefore the issues can be resolved by face-to-face contacts, or by temporary committees or groups. Following this line of reasoning it could be quite convincingly maintained that the smaller the group, the less the need for formal organization.

The above argument would be acceptable provided that, first, we were dealing with small groups and not with organizations

[1] Dunlop (1959, pp. 294-6). The points are: (i) The manager cannot any longer be dictatorial, but must use persuasion. (ii) The workers' council serves to discover potential managerial talents. (iii) It helps to commit workers fresh from farms to industrial discipline. (iv) It directs and contains dissatisfactions. (v) It reduces barriers between different groups within the factory. (vi) Decisions concerning profits teach the workers to be concerned with larger social issues. (vii) In a nationalized industry, the Yugoslav workers' council is an alternative to Soviet centralized management.

of hundreds of people, and, second, there were no other organizations within the Yugoslav enterprise. But this is not so. Moreover, the data indicate that the labour union especially was seeking to gain more influence and a more satisfactory definition of its role. It has already been pointed out that inasmuch as certain differences appear in any larger organization, informal groups will tend to adopt any of the existing organizations to serve as an organized framework for their protests.

Suppose that the existing organizations establish fairly harmonious relationships and that there is very little differentiation between those who manipulate concepts and those who manipulate things. Then could we expect tensions to be reduced? I would be inclined to accept this possibility, if the organizations existing in an enterprise were purely local and were independent of controls coming from outside centres. It will be remembered that the data have shown that the workers' council and management were the most independent structures, while the labour union, the youth organization, and probably also the League of Communists had more direction from outside. Since it is probable that these outside sources would send incompatible demands to their respective local organizations, it can be assumed theoretically that the result would be a certain tension on the local level.

Considering the Yugoslav system in its relation to outside influences, and remembering that all three secondary organizations within the enterprise tended to be more concerned with what were conveniently termed maintenance problems, then we see the workers' council system in a different light: apparently the national and communal organizations have concentrated their controls primarily upon the maintenance structure of the enterprise while the production structure has been granted more independence. In terms of urgency, most of the maintenance problems are not as pressing as the day-to-day production problems. Therefore the greater independence granted to the production structure has had beneficial effects. Essentially, the new workers' council legislation has primarily benefited management, giving it more freedom and room for initiative. On the

75

other hand, workers' labour unions have remained more dependent, not only upon management, but also upon direction from outside. On that count the workers have obtained less independence. Since management moves the enterprise forward by its decisions and innovations, and workers implement these decisions, Yugoslav production has not suffered but has experienced an upsurge.[1]

Possibly the above analysis has thrown the problem of industrial organization and industrial democracy into a somewhat new perspective. The findings have shown that the production and maintenance structures were given considerably different degrees of autonomy. In his conclusion, Dunlop makes a similar observation when referring to the 'compatibility of centralized political leadership and decentralized industrial-relations decisions at the work place' (1959, p. 306). The data and analysis in the present study demonstrate that the differential granting of autonomy has in fact been carried out within the enterprise itself in terms of the two structures, and not only in terms of separate political and economic institutions, as implied by Dunlop. Thus the Yugoslav enterprise today is a mixture of areas of autonomy – especially for management – and areas of controls – especially for labour. Though the workers are controlled by existing organizations in the enterprise on the one hand, on the other hand they are exposed to a great deal of information about the organization. 'The principle of publicity'[2] is probably unique, in most cases providing more information to employees in Yugoslavia than is supplied to their counterparts in Britain or the United States, or in the Soviet Union. Nevertheless, the findings from the two surveys have shown that, despite the publicity principle, most people in the enterprise did not greatly care to avail themselves the opportunities offered. The problem is: why not?

[1] See Organization for Economic Cooperation and Development, *Yugoslavia* (1962, pp. 41–2). Taking industrial output in 1953 as 100, in 1961 it reached 264. Agriculture was comparatively low, the corresponding indices being 1953, 106; 1960, 148.

[2] The term used by Gligorov (1961, p. 413).

Two possible explanations could be offered. First, that the absence of a genuine workers' organization has contributed to the lack of interest. Second, that in large modern organizations, whatever their political outlook, the majority of the members take little interest in administrative and managerial problems; current evidence on this point comes from countries on both sides of the iron curtain.

In concluding, it should be noted that the major function of both workers' councils, as I observed them, was informative and educational. Management was informed by worker members of the council about the attitudes of the rank and file, and worker members were exposed to managerial problems. In this respect both councils were quite successful. The worker members of the councils or their managing boards participated actively when personnel questions were discussed; their participation fell short of the professed definition of workers' management when technological developments as well as financial and marketing issues were discussed. Though Factory B was nearer the desired end than Factory A, in terms of decisions actually made, the two factories were not strikingly different. In both enterprises management got all the measures in which it was interested accepted by the workers' council.

References

ADAMOVITCH, A. (1956). Contemporary Yugoslav trade unions. *Highlights of Current Legislation and Activities in Mid-Europe.* Library of Congress, Mid-European Law Project, Vol. IV, No. 10, October, pp. 319–32. (Mimeographed.)

ADAMOVITCH, A. (1957). Industrial management in Yugoslavia. *Highlights of Current Legislation and Activities in Mid-Europe.* Library of Congress, Mid-European Law Project, Vol. V, Nos. 3 & 4, pp. 165–78. (Mimeographed.)

BENNETT, M. K. (1951). International disparities in consumption levels. *American Economic Review*, 41, 632–49.

BOGOSAVLJEVIĆ, M. & PEŠAKOVIĆ, M. (1959). *Workers' management of a factory in Yugoslavia.* Belgrade: Jugoslavija.

BREKIĆ, J. (1961). Pokretljivost u organima radničkog samoupravljanja. *Sociologija*, 3, No. 1, 63–9.

DELEON, A. (1956). *33 questions – 33 answers on workers' self-government in Yugoslavia.* Belgrade: Jugoslavija.

DJORDJEVIĆ, J. & PAŠIĆ, N. (1961). The communal self-government system in Yugoslavia. *International Social Science Journal*, 13, 389–407.

DUNLOP, J. T. (1959). *Industrial relations systems.* New York: Henry Holt.

Federal Statistical Institute (1959). *Statistical pocket-book of Yugoslavia 1959.* Belgrade.

GLIGOROV, K. (1961). The communal economy. *International Social Science Journal*, 13, 408–13.

HORVAT, B. & RAŠKOVIĆ, V. (1959). Workers' management in Yugoslavia: a comment. *Journal of Political Economy*, 67, 195.

Information Service Yugoslavia. The development of workers' self-government. RN 55–57–260–58–E. (Mimeographed.)

KARDELJ, E. (1957). Iskustva radničkih saveta. In *Zbornik o radničkom samoupravljanju.* Belgrade: Rad.

References

KERR, C., DUNLOP, J. T., HARBISON, F. H. & MYERS, C. A. (1960). *Industrialism and industrial man: the problems of labor and management in economic growth.* Cambridge, Mass.: Harvard University Press.

KOLAJA, J. (1960). *A Polish factory: a case study of workers' participation in decision-making.* Lexington: University of Kentucky Press.

KOLAJA, J. (1961). A Yugoslav workers' council. *Human Organization,* 20, 27–31.

KOVAČ, P. (1958). *Workers' management in Yugoslavia.* Belgrade: Jugoslavija.

KOVAČ, P. & MILJEVIĆ, DJ. (1958). *Samoupravljanje proizvodjača u privredi.* Belgrade: Savremena Administracja.

MACURA, M. (1961). Basic statistics on the Yugoslav commune. *International Social Science Journal,* 3, 431.

MATIĆ, S., POČEK, M. & BOSANAC, G. *Aktivnost radnih ljudi u samoupravljanju radnom organizacijom: jedan pokušaj istraživanja na području komune Varaždin.* Zagreb: Institut za Društveno Upravljanje NRH.

NIČKOVIĆ, R. (1961). Ispitivanje predznanja neposrednih proizvodjača u oblasti društveno-ekonomskog obrazovanja. *Sociologija,* 3, No. 1, 88–95.

Organization for Economic Cooperation and Development (1962). *Yugoslavia.* Paris.

POČEK, M. (1960). Funkcionalna mobilnost u organima radničkog samoupravljanja. *Ekonomski Pregled,* 2, 723–38.

Program Związku Komunistów Jugosławii (1959). Paris: Instytut Literacki.

RADOSAVLJEVIĆ, M. (1961). Radnici o nekim pitanjima raspodele čistog prihoda i ličnog dohodka. *Sociologija,* 3, No. 1, 70–8.

RAŠKOVIĆ, V. (1961). Osvrt na neke 'ocene' na zapadu o našem radničkom samoupravljanju. *Sociologija,* 3, No. 1, 142–52.

ROOSEVELT, E. (1958). *On my own.* New York: Harper.

ROSTOW, W. W. (1960). *The stages of economic growth: a non-communist manifesto.* London: Cambridge University Press.

SINADINOVIĆ, J. (1959). Prvi pokušaji empiriskih istraživanja radničkog samoupravljanja. *Sociologija,* 1, No. 1, 141–52.

SIROTOVIĆ, J. (1954). *Novi privredni sistem FNRJ-osnove, organizacioni oblici i metode upravljanja.* Zagreb: Naprijed.

STURMTHAL, A. (1964). *Workers' councils.* Cambridge, Mass: Harvard University Press.

ŠUŠNIĆ, D. (1961). Neki rezultati analize sadržaja dnevnog lista Borba. *Sociologija,* 3, No. 1, 110–19.

TANIĆ, Z. (1961). Neke tendencije u dosadašnjem radu radničkih saveta. *Sociologija*, **3**, No. 2, 101–19.

TANNENBAUM, A. S. & KAHN, R. L. (1958). *Participation in union locals.* Evanston, Ill.: Row, Peterson.

TITO, J. B. (1959). Govor Druga Tita, in *Četvrti kongres Saveza Sindikata Jugoslavije Beograd 23–26 aprila 1959 godine.* Belgrade: Rad. Pp. 9–16.

WINIARSKI, Ł. (1954). List z Jugosławii. *Kultura* (Paris), January–February. 1/75–2/76, 114–24.

Yugoslav facts and views (1957). Statute of enterprises in Yugoslavia, No. 24, 13 May. (Mimeographed.)

ŽUPANOV, J. & MARJANOVIĆ, I. (1960). *Ekonomske jedinice kao socijalne grupe.* Zagreb: Centar za Obrazovanje Rukovodnih Kadrova u Privredi.

Index

adjustments, functional, 70f
agriculture, 3n
Algeria, x n
associations, professional, 4
attitudes, management and non-management, 38ff
autonomy
  and control, mixture, 76
  of organizations, 65f

chambers, industrial, 4
collectivity, and organizations, relations, 68f
collegium, 15
committees, of workers' council, 27f
commune
  as self-governmental unit, 2
  see also workers' council
commune, *see* enterprise
communication
  failure of, 40, 71
  workers' council and, 64
competition, 4
Council of Producers, 3 28
credit control, 4

decentralization, 12
decision-making, locus of, 12
director, functions of, 5, 6
discussion
  degree of participation in, 19ff, 23, 50f
  topics of, 24, 25
division of labour, between organizations, 66f

egoism, organizational, 71
enterprise

and commune, relation, 3 n
and Council of Producers, 63
and society, relation, 4f, 9
workers' feeling of ownership in, 40f

Factory A
  attitude of workers, 57ff
  description, 14
  income, 16
  organization, 15
  personnel, 14
Factory B
  description, 14
  income, 16
  organization, 15f
  personnel, 15
Federal Council of Producers, 9
Federation of Yugoslav Communists, 2n

group rewards, 10f

income
  national, factors in, 3n
  range of, 32
  workers', 10
individuals, problems of, 27
interest rates, fixing, 9

labour unions, 5, 29ff
  activities of, 31
  attendance at meetings, 31
  committee, meeting, 53f
  degree of influence, 34
  functions of, 29, 67
  meetings, 52ff
  turnover, 29

83